W9-BYR-204

Flip & Fuse quilts

Transform Your Appliqué!

12 Fun Projects
Easy Foolproof Technique

Marcia Harmening

C&T PUBLISHING

Text copyright © 2015 by Marcia Harmening

Photography and artwork copyright © 2015 by C&T Publishing, Inc.

Publisher: Amy Marson

Creative Director: Gailen Runge

Art Director / Cover Designer: Kristy Zacharias

Editor: S. Michele Fry

Technical Editors: Alison M. Schmidt and Amanda Siegfried

Book Designer: April Mostek

Production Coordinator: Jenny Davis and Freesia Pearson Blizard

Production Editor: Alice Mace Nakanishi

Illustrator: Valyrie Gillum

Photo Assistant: Mary Peyton Peppo

Style photography by Nissa Brehmer and **instructional photography** by Diane Pedersen, unless otherwise noted

Published by C&T Publishing, Inc., P.O. Box 1456, Lafayette, CA 94549

Library of Congress Cataloging-in-Publication Data

Harmening, Marcia.

Flip & fuse quilts : :12 fun projects - easy foolproof technique --transform your appliqué! / Marcia Harmening.

pages cm

ISBN 978-1-61745-140-9 (soft cover)

1. Appliqué--Patterns. 2. Quilting. 3. Fusible materials in sewing. I. Title. II. Title: Flip and fuse quilts.

TT779.H364 2015

746.44'5041--dc23

2015017926

Printed in China

10 9 8 7 6 5 4 3 2 1

Contents

Dedication

Photo by Darby Ann Photography

For Mike—my loving rock in life who makes me a better person. His stead-fast ways, incomparable integrity, and self-sacrificing spirit have made our marriage and family life raising Ali, Kenny, and Robin in both Alaska and Nevada an adventurous and rewarding journey. I must have won the marital lottery to be married to a man who truly believes a happy wife equals a happy life. Thank you for encouraging me to chase my dreams.

Acknowledgments

A huge thank-you to my mom, Elaine Jones, who has the kindest, most receptive ears and an abundance of patience as I bounce ideas, designs, and patterns off her ad nauseam. Mom is a delightful travel companion to quilt shows, as is her "other daughter," Jane Olsen—the most amazing friend ever!

Gratitude is also extended to Brenda Henning of Bear Baw Productions, who unselfishly paved the way for me in the quilting world by freely sharing her knowledge, wisdom, and experience.

Inspiration comes from my dad, Bob Jones, who astonishes me with his energy and enthusiasm for painting. My friend Diane Chilimpis was the catalyst for my transition from quilting as a hobby to quilting as a designer and pattern publisher.

And quilting just would not be a party without the support of my dear quilting friends—Heather Banks, Lisa Bauer, Lela Benson, Sally Boussios, Traci Deam, Cindy Grove, Dana Hyams, Lauren Jackson, Janet McWorkman, Heidi Uselmann, Terri Wangstom, Megan Wanless, Teresa Wavra, and my favorite "Bloomin' Dozen," "Midnight Sun," "Pine Quilters," and "Threads of Friendship" ladies.

Introduction

I enjoy beautiful geometric quilts; however, add a splash of appliqué to any project and I am in love! The softening touch of gentle curves that appliqué creates takes quilts to a whole new artistic level.

Unfortunately, many quilters are terrified of the "A" word. They are scared off by the thought of needlework, or they believe appliqué simply takes too much time. Well, never fear! This book opens the door for every quilter to quickly and confidently march right into the wonderful world of appliqué. No tedious hand needlework is involved; all turned-edge appliqué pieces are sewn on by machine to significantly speed up the process.

While the Flip & Fuse technique used in this book has been floating around in the quilting world for a while, this easy pathway to appliqué is highly underutilized. I want quilters to know they can boldly add their own personal stamp to any quilt and transform a mere project into a work of art.

As a quilter, I absolutely love this quote from St. Francis of Assisi: "He who works with his hands is a laborer. He who works with his hands and his head is a craftsman. He who works with his hands and his head and his heart is an artist."

I will never be a great painter or sculptor or architect, but I feel very fortunate to have found a creative niche that brings me such joy as I work with my hands, my head, and my heart. I am honored to share my passion for quilting with all my fellow artists.

Happy quilting!

—Marcia

The Wonderful World of Flip & Fuse Appliqué

With this technique, all your appliqué edges are turned under and finished without the necessity of painstaking, tedious needlework by hand. The secret to this magical method is lightweight fusible interfacing!

How Flip & Fuse Works

1. Choose a product to use (see Two Fusible Product Options, page 7):

- **Wash-Away Appliqué Sheets (by C&T Publishing)**
  Cut the appliqué fabric pieces the size indicated in the chart for the quilt you are making. Test your printer settings first and be sure to print on the nonfusible side of the sheet. Print the indicated number of appliqué sheets. Roughly cut the shapes apart.

.... *or* ....

- **911FF Fusible Featherweight interfacing (by Pellon)** *or* **Wash-Away Appliqué Roll (by C&T Publishing)**
  Cut the appliqué fabric pieces and the fusible interfacing pieces the size indicated in the chart for the quilt you are making. Trace the indicated number of appliqué shapes onto the nonfusible side of the interfacing. Any nonsymmetrical shapes have already been flipped for the fusible appliqué.

2. Pin the fusible interfacing on top of each fabric piece so that the glue side of the fusible interfacing is toward the right side of the fabric. The side with the printed or traced line should be on top.

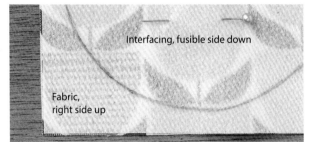

Pellon 911FF with traced line

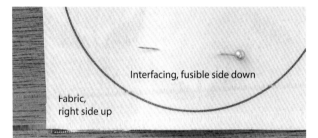

C&T Appliqué Sheet with printed line

3. Sew the 2 pieces together on the line. Repeat for all the shapes.

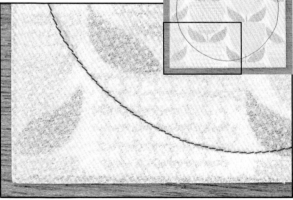

Tip When the stitching line is a tight V shape, it will be easier to flip the appliqué right side out if you take 1 straight stitch across the base of the V, making a V with a flat bottom instead of a sharp point.

4. Trim the excess fabric and interfacing ⅛" beyond the stitching line of each piece. Cut a long slit in the fusible interfacing, parallel to the longest edge of the shape; stop at least ½"

from the stitching. Be careful not to cut the fabric underneath. There is no need to clip the curves because the seam allowance is only ⅛".

5. Turn each unit right side out by pulling the right side of the fabric through the slit in the interfacing. The fusible side of the interfacing should now be on the outside. Stick a blunt instrument or your fingers through the slit in the interfacing and gently smooth out the seam around the edges by finger-pressing until you are pleased with the shape of the unit. Do not use an iron to press the edges flat!

6. Arrange the shapes as directed on the background block. Position as many pieces as possible at a time. Follow the manufacturer's instructions to carefully fuse the shape(s)

onto the background. Use an up-and-down motion so the pieces don't shift. Depending on your iron, you may need to fuse a single layer at a time for some projects with overlapping pieces.

7. Stitch each piece to the background block using a narrow zigzag stitch, a buttonhole stitch, or even a straight stitch along the edges.

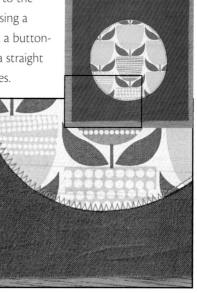

Straight stitch

Narrow zigzag stitch

Buttonhole stitch

NOTE _____

I use a clear .004 nylon monofilament thread on the top of my machine and keep a regular cotton thread in the bobbin. I lower the top tension slightly so the bobbin thread doesn't peek through to the top of the quilt. For dark fabrics, consider using smoke-colored nylon thread.

If you are using color-coordinated threads, skip around to stitch around all the pieces with the first color, then change only the top thread to stitch the pieces in the next color, and so on until all the pieces are appliquéd.

Two Fusible Product Options

I like two different lightweight fusible products:

- **911FF Fusible Featherweight interfacing (by Pellon)** is available as 20″-wide yardage in 40-yard bolts (white) and 15-yard bolts (charcoal).

- **Wash-Away Appliqué Sheets (by C&T Publishing)** is available in packs of 25 printer-ready 8½″ × 11″ sheets that fit in a standard printer.

How to Pick Your Product

Pellon Advantage

Pellon's 911FF Fusible Featherweight interfacing is a winner because it costs less. By buying this product on the 20″-wide bolt you are guaranteed to save money and have a more efficient use of the product. However, you will need to trace all the shapes by hand, which takes time.

C&T Advantage

C&T's Wash-Away Appliqué Sheets are a winner because they save time. Simply put the 8½″ × 11″ sheets in your inkjet printer and make the number of copies indicated in the pattern. No time-consuming template tracing by hand. However, varying template shapes make it difficult to maximize the usage of each page and will cost more money.

C&T's product also comes in 14″ × 10-yard rolls. If you try both products and find this is your preference, you can use the tracing method with the larger Wash-Away Appliqué Roll product. More yardage will be needed than with the wider Pellon interfacing.

Your product selection boils down to time versus money. Every pattern in this book provides yardage/sheet requirements and preparation instructions for using the bolt and the C&T printable sheets. Select the product that best suits your needs.

Tools for Turning

Each "flipped" appliqué piece needs to have the edges pushed out gently before it is ready to be fused onto the quilt top. A variety of simple tools will get the job done— That Purple Thang, the tip of a mechanical pencil with the lead retracted, a blunt toothpick, or even a chopstick.

However, my favorite tool is a Phillips-head screwdriver with a shank diameter of about ⅛″. It is narrow enough to push out points on appliqué shapes yet blunt enough that you don't have to worry about poking a hole through the fusible interfacing. Also, the four ridges on the X-shaped head help slightly grab the fusible interfacing and fabric, allowing you to easily maneuver and finesse your pieces into the proper shape. Make a quick trip to your hardware store or out to the garage and you are ready to go!

Note: Flower-handled or bright pink screwdrivers possess better odds of remaining with your sewing supplies instead of migrating to the garage tools.

Level of Difficulty

Each project is assigned a level of difficulty.

- **Level 1**   These quilts contain simple piecing and use large Flip & Fuse appliqué pieces, which are easy to turn right side out.

- **Level 2**   These quilts require more time piecing background blocks or use smaller Flip & Fuse appliqué pieces that take more time to turn right side out.

- **Level 3**   Only two quilts in the book are Level 3. *Hoppy* (page 49) has easy piecing but includes appliqué pieces that require a little finesse to turn right side out. *Crossroads* (page 65) has easy Flip & Fuse appliqué but features more difficult piecing.

Summer Breeze

Finished blocks: Flower 10″ × 10″, leaf 10″ × 5″

Finished quilt: Throw 56″ × 71″ (size shown)

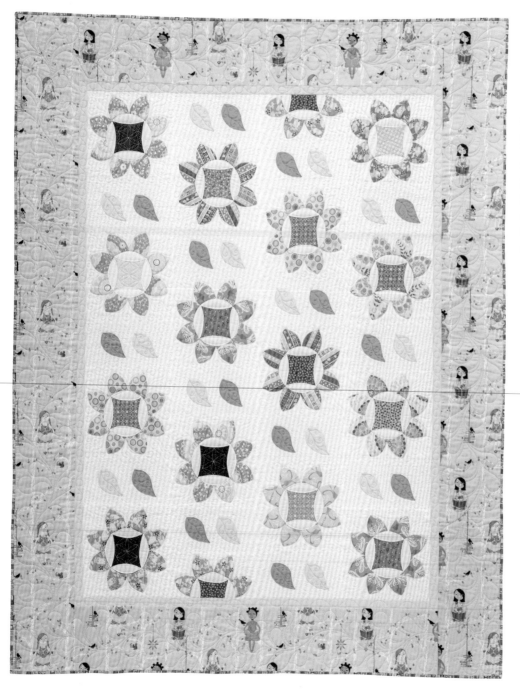

This quilt requires no block piecing. Simply play with pretty fabrics to flip and fuse flowers and leaves to make the blocks for this quilt top.

Border fabric: *Quiet Time by Tamara Kate for Michael Miller Fabrics*
Other fabrics: *Courtesy of Michael Miller Fabrics*

FABRIC REQUIREMENTS

Yardage is based on 42" fabric width. An assortment of fabrics are used for the flowers. Refer to the suggested number of fabrics and associated yardage for *each*.

	Baby 46" × 56"	Throw 56" × 71"	Twin 66" × 86"	Full 86" × 96"	Queen 96" × 96"	King 106" × 96"
Number of blocks:						
Leaf blocks	8	14	23	37	43	48
Flower blocks	7	14	22	35	40	45
Half-flower blocks	2	2	3	5	5	6
Fabrics:						
White background	1¾ yards	2½ yards	4 yards	5¾ yards	6½ yards	7½ yards
Light leaves and inner border	⅜ yard	½ yard	¾ yard	1 yard	1¼ yards	1¼ yards
Dark leaves	¼ yard	¼ yard	⅓ yard	½ yard	⅔ yard	⅔ yard
Flower fabrics	3 fabrics, ⅜ yard *each*	6 fabrics, ⅜ yard *each*	9 fabrics, ⅜ yard *each*	7 fabrics, ⅝ yard *each*	8 fabrics, ⅝ yard *each*	9 fabrics, ⅝ yard *each*
Outer border (if directional print)	1⅔ yards (2⅛ yards)	2⅛ yards (2¾ yards)	2½ yards (3⅛ yards)	2¾ yards (3⅝ yards)	3 yards (4 yards)	3⅛ yards (4 yards)
Backing	3 yards	3¾ yards	5½ yards	8 yards	9 yards	9 yards
Binding	½ yard	½ yard	⅝ yard	¾ yard	¾ yard	¾ yard
Batting	54" × 64"	64" × 79"	74" × 94"	94" × 104"	104" × 104"	114" × 104"
Fusible interfacing (choose one):*						
C&T Appliqué Sheets	16 sheets	28 sheets	44 sheets	70 sheets	79 sheets	90 sheets
Pellon 911FF	3 yards	5 yards	7½ yards	12½ yards	14 yards	15 yards

* For fusible interfacing comparisons, refer to How to Pick Your Product (page 7).

CUTTING DIRECTIONS

WOF = width of fabric; LOF = length of fabric

WHITE BACKGROUND:

	Baby	Throw	Twin	Full	Queen	King
Cut 10½" × WOF strips.	4	6	10	15	17	20
Subcut 10½" × 10½" squares for flower blocks.	7	14	22	35	40	45
Subcut 10½" × 5½" rectangles for leaf blocks and half-flower blocks.	10	16	26	42	48	54
Cut 4" × WOF strips for appliqué shapes.	2	3	5	8	9	10
Subcut 4" × 2" rectangles.	34	62	97	155	175	198

LIGHT LEAVES:

	Baby	Throw	Twin	Full	Queen	King
Cut 4½" × WOF strips.	1	1	2	3	4	4
Subcut 4½" × 3" rectangles.	8	14	23	37	43	48
Cut 1½" × WOF strips for inner border.	4	5	7	8	9	9

DARK LEAVES:

	Baby	Throw	Twin	Full	Queen	King
Cut 4½" × WOF strips.	1	1	2	3	4	4
Subcut 4½" × 3" rectangles.	8	14	23	37	43	48

	Baby	Throw	Twin	Full	Queen	King
Cut 3″ × WOF strips from *each* fabric.	2	2	2	4	4	4
Subcut *total* of 3″ × 3½″ rectangles. *(You will need sets of 8 matching 3″ × 3½″ rectangles for each flower and 4 matching 3″ × 3½″ rectangles for each half-flower.)*	64	120	188	300	340	384
Cut 5½″ × WOF strips from *each* fabric.	1	1	1	1	1	1
Subcut *total* of 5½″ × 5½″ squares.	9	16	25	40	45	51

	Baby	Throw	Twin	Full	Queen	King
If nondirectional print:						
Cut 7½″ × LOF strips.	4	4	4	4	4	4
If directional print:						
Cut 7½″ × WOF strips for top and bottom borders.	3	4	4	5	6	6
Cut 7½″ × remaining LOF strips for side borders.	2	2	2	2	2	2

	Baby	Throw	Twin	Full	Queen	King
Cut 2¼″ × WOF strips.	6	7	8	10	10	11

· C&T Wash-Away Appliqué Sheets

Follow the manufacturer's instructions to print the indicated number of Summer Breeze pattern sheets (pages 76 and 77) onto the *nonfusible* side of 8½″ × 11″ sheets of interfacing, using your inkjet printer. You will have extra fusible leaf and petal shapes.

Note: If using C&T Wash-Away Appliqué Roll, follow the instructions for Pellon interfacing (at right).

C&T Appliqué Sheets	Baby	Throw	Twin	Full	Queen	King
Sheet 1	9	16	25	40	45	51
Sheet 2	7	12	19	30	34	39

·········· *or* ··········

· Pellon 911FF Fusible Featherweight interfacing

Cut the interfacing into the indicated sizes and quantities of pieces. Trace 1 shape from the pattern sheets (pages 76 and 77) onto the *nonfusible* side of each corresponding interfacing piece.

Pellon 911FF	Baby	Throw	Twin	Full	Queen	King
Flower centers: 5½″ × 5½″	9	16	25	40	45	51
Melons: 2″ × 4″	34	62	97	155	175	198
Leaves: 3″ × 4½″	16	28	46	74	86	96
Petals: 3″ × 3½″	64	120	188	300	340	384

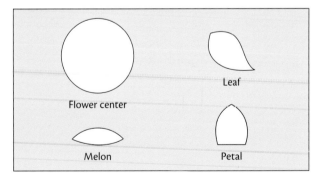

Flower center

Leaf

Melon

Petal

Flip & Fuse *For detailed instructions on this method, refer to How Flip & Fuse Works (page 5).*

1. If you are using C&T Wash-Away Appliqué Sheets, cut apart the Center, Melon, Leaf, and Petal patterns. Leave at least ⅛″ beyond the drawn lines.

2. Place each of the center fusible interfacing pieces on a 5½″ × 5½″ square of flower fabric so the fusible side of the interfacing piece is facing the right side of the fabric.

Fabric right side up
Interfacing glue side down

3. Sew on the lines.

4. Trim the excess fabric and fusible interfacing ⅛″ beyond the sewn lines.

5. Cut a slit in the interfacing of each piece, being careful not to cut the fabric.

Trim fabric and interfacing ⅛″ beyond stitching.
Cut a slit in the interfacing only.

6. Flip the units right side out. Insert a blunt tool inside the cut in the interfacing and gently push out the points and edges of each unit. Run the tool along the edges of each piece and finger-press the edges where the fabric and fusible interfacing meet. Set the prepared pieces aside until the blocks are constructed.

7. Repeat Steps 2–6 for the melons, leaves, and petals, using the appropriate fabric as listed.

- Place the melon fusible interfacing pieces on 2″ × 4″ rectangles of white background fabric.

- Place the leaf fusible interfacing pieces on 3″ × 4½″ rectangles of light green and dark green fabrics.

- Place the petal fusible interfacing pieces on 3″ × 3½″ rectangles of various flower fabrics.

NOTE
You do not need to sew along the base of the petals because a flower circle will cover the raw edges of these pieces. You do not need to cut a slit in the interfacing either; simply turn the unit right side out through the unsewn base.

Prepared pieces	Baby	Throw	Twin	Full	Queen	King
Flower centers	9	16	25	40	45	51
Light green leaves	8	14	23	37	43	48
Dark green leaves	8	14	23	37	43	48
White melons	34	62	97	155	175	198
Flower petals	64	120	188	300	340	384

Leaf Block Construction

1. Place a prepared light leaf and a prepared dark leaf on a 5½″ × 10½″ background rectangle. Use a hot iron to fuse in place. Repeat to make the required number of blocks.

NOTE
About half the blocks have the dark leaf on the left; the remaining blocks have the light leaf on the left.

2. Using clear thread on top, sew the edges of the fused leaves to the background blocks using a blanket stitch or a zigzag stitch. Slightly lower the top tension on your machine to make sure the bobbin thread does not show on top.

Leaf blocks	Baby	Throw	Twin	Full	Queen	King
Dark leaf on left	4	6	11	18	21	24
Light leaf on left	4	8	12	19	22	24

Flower Block Construction

Whole Flower Blocks

Select 8 matching prepared flower petals, 1 flower center, and 4 melon pieces. Fold the block in half both vertically and horizontally to find the center of the 10½" × 10½" background block. Place the flower center in the middle of the block. Hold the flower center in place while you slip each petal base ¼" under the center so the raw edges are covered. Follow the manufacturer's instructions to fuse the flower center and flower petals in place with a hot iron. Add white melon pieces on top and fuse in place. Repeat to make the required number of blocks.

Half-Flower Blocks

1. Select 4 matching prepared flower petals, 1 flower center, and 3 melon pieces. Arrange them to create a half-flower block on a background 5½" × 10½" rectangle. Make sure the 2 petals closest to what would be the center of the flower are placed ¼" in from the edge so they are not caught in the seam allowance. Use a hot iron and fuse in place. Use an appliqué pressing sheet or Silicone Release Paper (by C&T Publishing) to protect your iron and ironing board from fusible residue. Trim the part of the circle and melons that extends beyond the edge of the block. Repeat to make the required number of blocks.

2. Using clear thread on top, sew the flower pieces to the background blocks in the same manner in which you did the leaves.

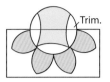

Trim the pieces that extend beyond the block along the red line.

Blocks	Baby	Throw	Twin	Full	Queen	King
Whole flowers	7	14	22	35	40	45
Half-flowers	2	2	3	5	5	6

Quilt Top Construction

1. Lay out the flower blocks, half-flower blocks, and leaf blocks as shown for the selected quilt size. Sew the blocks into columns. Press all the seams toward the leaf blocks.

2. Sew the columns together to form the quilt top center. Press all the seams in the same direction.

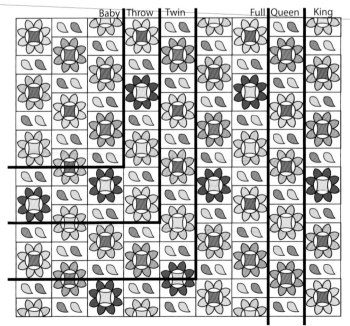

Quilt assembly
Note: Your quilt may have more or less fabric variety than shown here, due to the size you chose.

Borders

1. To make the inner border, diagonally piece the inner border strips together to form a continuous strip. Trim the seam allowances to ¼" and press to one side.

2. Measure the quilt vertically through the center. Cut 2 inner border strips to the needed length for the side borders. Attach the side borders to the quilt. Press the seam allowances toward the inner border.

3. Measure the quilt horizontally through the center. Cut 2 inner border strips to the needed length for the top and bottom borders. Attach the top and bottom borders to the quilt. Press all the seams toward the inner border.

4. To make the outer border, follow the instructions for nondirectional or directional print fabric:

For nondirectional print Repeat Steps 2 and 3 to measure the quilt top and cut, attach, and press first the side outer borders and then the top and bottom outer borders. Press all the seams toward the outer border.

For directional print Repeat Step 2 to measure the quilt and trim the 2 *lengthwise* border strips to the needed length. Sew to the sides of the quilt. Repeat Step 1 to piece the widthwise border together. Measure the quilt horizontally and cut 2 borders to the needed length for the top and bottom of the quilt. Attach the top and bottom borders. Press all the seams toward the outer border.

Quilting Ideas

Laurie Vandergriff mimicked the melon shapes to create a flower design in the middle of the flower. She also used beautiful swirls in the background to capture the feel of a light summer breeze.

Finishing

Layer the backing, batting, and quilt top. Baste and quilt as desired. Diagonally piece the 2¼"-wide binding strips together to form a continuous strip. Trim the seam allowances to ¼" and press to one side. Press the strip in half with wrong sides together. Attach to the quilt.

Alternate colorway

Petal Patch

Difficulty: Level 2

Finished block: 10″ × 10″

Finished quilt: Twin 66″ × 86″ (size shown)

The fused melon shapes create the look of intricate curved piecing without all the work. This same melon shape makes it easy to cut curves for an elegant border.

Border fabric: *Gypsy Girl Wishing Well Blue Rose by Lily Ashbury for Moda*

FABRIC REQUIREMENTS

Yardage is based on 42" fabric width. The same blue fabric is used for all the blocks; however, for all quilts larger than the baby size, an assortment of pink, green, and yellow fabrics is used to give the quilt added interest. Please refer to the suggested number of fabrics and associated yardage for *each*.

	Baby 36" × 46"	Throw 56" × 66"	Twin 66" × 86"	Full 86" × 96"	Queen 96" × 96"	King 106" × 96"
Number of blocks	6	20	35	56	64	72
Fabrics:						
Blue	⅜ yard	1 yard	1½ yards	2⅛ yards	2⅓ yards	2¾ yards
Yellows	1 fabric, ¼ yard	4 fabrics, ¼ yard *each*	6 fabrics, ¼ yard *each*	5 fabrics, ⅜ yard *each*	6 fabrics, ⅜ yard *each*	6 fabrics, ⅜ yard *each*
Pinks	1 fabric, ¼ yard	4 fabrics, ¼ yard *each*	6 fabrics, ¼ yard *each*	5 fabrics, ⅜ yard *each*	6 fabrics, ⅜ yard *each*	6 fabrics, ⅜ yard *each*
Greens	1 fabric, ¼ yard	3 fabrics, ¼ yard *each*	6 fabrics, ¼ yard *each*	5 fabrics, ⅜ yard *each*	6 fabrics, ⅜ yard *each*	6 fabrics, ⅜ yard *each*
White	1 yard	2 yards	3 yards	4½ yards	5 yards	5⅝ yards
Magenta	¼ yard	¼ yard	⅜ yard	½ yard	½ yard	½ yard
Border fabric (if directional print)	1¼ yards (1½ yards)	1¾ yards (2⅝ yards)	2¼ yards (3¼ yards)	2½ yards (3⅞ yards)	3 yards (4 yards)	3¼ yards (4⅛ yards)
Backing	2⅝ yards	3¾ yards	5⅜ yards	8 yards	9 yards	9 yards
Bias binding	¾ yard	⅞ yard	1 yard	1 yard	1⅛ yards	1⅛ yards
Batting	44" × 54"	64" × 74"	74" × 94"	94" × 104"	104" × 104"	114" × 104"
Fusible interfacing (choose one):*						
C&T Appliqué Sheets	9 sheets	25 sheets	41 sheets	64 sheets	72 sheets	81 sheets
Pellon 911FF	2 yards	4½ yards	7 yards	10½ yards	11½ yards	13 yards

* For fusible interfacing comparisons, refer to How to Pick Your Product (page 7).

CUTTING DIRECTIONS   *WOF = width of fabric; LOF = length of fabric*

BLUE FABRIC:

	Baby	Throw	Twin	Full	Queen	King
Cut 4½" × WOF strips.	2	5	9	14	16	18
Subcut 4½" × 2½" rectangles.	24	80	140	224	256	288

FROM *EACH* YELLOW, PINK, AND GREEN FABRIC:

Each block uses 4 squares 4½" × 4½" and 1 square 2½" × 2½" of identical fabric.

	Baby	Throw	Twin	Full	Queen	King
Cut 4½" × WOF strips.	1	1	1	2	2	2
Subcut 4½" × 4½" squares.	8	8	8	16	16	16
Cut 2½" × WOF strips.	1	1	1	1	1	1
Subcut 2½" × 2½" squares.	2	2	2	4	4	4

TOTAL YELLOW PIECES NEEDED:

	Baby	Throw	Twin	Full	Queen	King
4½″ × 4½″ squares	8	28	44	76	84	96
2½″ × 2½″ squares	2	7	11	19	21	24

TOTAL PINK PIECES NEEDED:

	Baby	Throw	Twin	Full	Queen	King
4½″ × 4½″ squares	8	28	48	76	88	96
2½″ × 2½″ squares	2	7	12	19	22	24

TOTAL GREEN PIECES NEEDED:

	Baby	Throw	Twin	Full	Queen	King
4½″ × 4½″ squares	8	24	48	72	84	96
2½″ × 2½″ squares	2	6	12	18	21	24

WHITE FABRIC:

	Baby	Throw	Twin	Full	Queen	King
Cut 4½″ × WOF strips.	5	13	21	32	36	41
Subcut 4½″ × 10½″ rectangles.	17	49	82	127	144	161

MAGENTA FABRIC:

	Baby	Throw	Twin	Full	Queen	King
Cut 2½″ × WOF strips.	1	2	3	5	6	6
Subcut 2½″ × 2½″ squares.	12	30	48	72	81	90

BORDER:

	Baby	Throw	Twin	Full	Queen	King
If nondirectional print:						
Cut 8½″ × LOF strips.	4	4	4	4	4	4
If directional print:						
Cut 8½″ × WOF strips for top and bottom borders.	2	4	4	5	6	6
Cut 8½″ × LOF strips for side borders.	2	2	2	2	2	2

BINDING:

When you are ready to make and apply the bias binding, refer to Continuous Bias Binding (page 19).

FUSIBLE INTERFACING (CHOOSE ONE):

- **C&T Wash-Away Appliqué Sheets**

Follow the manufacturer's instructions to print the indicated number of Petal Patch pattern sheets (page 78) onto the *nonfusible* side of 8½″ × 11″ sheets of interfacing, using your inkjet printer.

Note: If using C&T Wash-Away Appliqué Roll, follow the instructions for Pellon interfacing (below).

C&T Appliqué Sheets	Baby	Throw	Twin	Full	Queen	King
Number of copies	17	49	82	127	144	161

························· *or* ·························

- **Pellon 911FF Fusible Featherweight interfacing**

Cut the interfacing into the indicated sizes and quantities of pieces. Trace 1 shape (page 78) onto the *nonfusible* side of each corresponding interfacing piece.

Pellon	Baby	Throw	Twin	Full	Queen	King
Circles: 2½″ × 2½″	12	30	48	72	81	90
Melons: 4½″ × 10½″	17	49	82	127	144	161

Flip & Fuse

For detailed instructions on this method, refer to How Flip & Fuse Works (page 5).

1. If you are using C&T Wash-Away Appliqué Sheets, cut apart the Melon and Circle patterns. Leave at least ⅛″ beyond the drawn lines.

2. Place each of the circle fusible interfacing pieces on a 2½″ × 2½″ magenta fabric piece so the fusible side of the interfacing piece is facing the right side of the fabric.

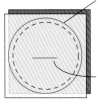

Fabric right side up

Interfacing glue side down

3. Sew on the drawn lines.

4. Trim the excess fabric and fusible interfacing ⅛″ beyond the sewn lines.

5. Cut a slit in the fusible interfacing of each piece, being careful not to cut the fabric.

Trim fabric and interfacing ⅛″ beyond stitching.

Cut a slit in the interfacing only.

6. Flip the units right side out. Insert a blunt instrument inside the cut in the interfacing and gently push out the points and edges of each unit. Run the blunt instrument along the edges of each piece and finger-press the edges where the fabric and fusible interfacing meet. Set the prepared pieces aside until the quilt top is constructed.

7. Place each of the melon fusible interfacing pieces on a 4½″ × 10½″ white rectangle so the fusible side of the interfacing piece is facing the right side of the fabric. Prepare the melons in the same manner as the circles, following Steps 3–6.

Block Construction

1. Sew a blue 2½″ × 4½″ rectangle to each side of a yellow 2½″ × 2½″ square. Press the seams toward the blue rectangles.

Make 1.

2. Select 4 yellow 4½″ × 4½″ squares that match the 2½″ × 2½″ yellow square used in Step 1. Sew a yellow 4½″ × 4½″ square to each side of a blue 2½″ × 4½″ rectangle. Press the seams toward the blue rectangles. Repeat to make a second unit.

Make 2.

3. Sew a Step 2 unit to each side of the Step 1 unit. Press the seams toward the Step 2 units.

4. Repeat Steps 1–3 to make the remaining yellow blocks.

5. Repeat Steps 1–4 to construct the pink and green blocks.

Blocks	Baby	Throw	Twin	Full	Queen	King
Yellow	2	7	11	19	21	24
Pink	2	7	12	19	22	24
Green	2	6	12	18	21	24

Quilt Top Construction

1. Lay out the yellow, pink, and green blocks as shown in the quilt assembly diagram for the selected quilt size.

2. Sew the blocks into rows. Press the seam allowances of the even rows in one direction and the seam allowances of the odd rows in the other direction.

3. Sew the rows together to form the quilt top center. Press all the seams in the same direction.

4. Refer to *Summer Breeze*, Borders (page 13), to measure, trim, and attach first the side borders and then the top and bottom borders to the quilt top.

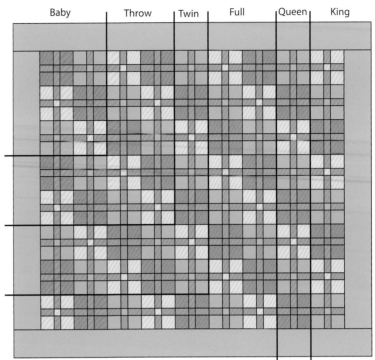

| Baby | Throw | Twin | Full | Queen | King |

Quilt assembly

Note: Your quilt may have more fabric variety than shown here, due to the size you chose.

Appliqué

1. Refer to the appliqué placement diagram to place the prepared melon pieces and then the circle pieces on the quilt top. Follow the manufacturer's instructions to fuse in place, using a hot iron.

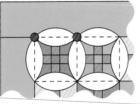

Appliqué placement

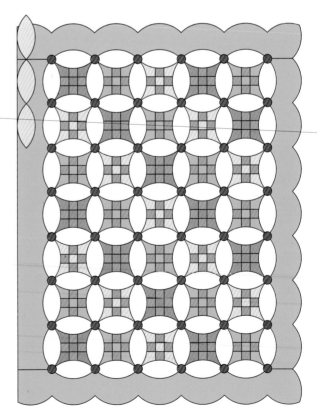

2. Using clear thread on top, sew the edge of each fused piece to the quilt top using a blanket stitch or a zigzag stitch. Slightly lower the top tension on your machine to make sure the bobbin thread does not show on top.

3. Trace the Melon pattern onto a piece of freezer paper or template plastic. Cut out the traced melon.

4. Use the Melon template to mark and trim the edges of the quilt. Simply line up the long side of the template with the edge of the quilt, directly across from a fused melon shape. The Melon template will extend beyond the border edges in the corners.

Quilting Ideas

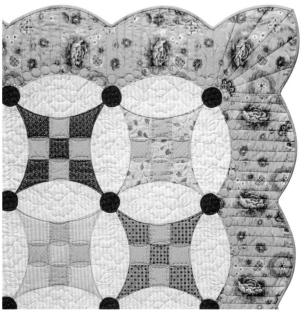

Laurie Vandergriff beautifully echoed the roses from the border in the quilting on the white melon pieces. She opted to quilt small circles inside the magenta circles. She continued the circle theme into the first part of the border and made the border pop with straight lines extending outward.

Alternate colorway

Finishing

Layer the backing, batting, and quilt top. Baste and quilt as desired.

Continuous Bias Binding

Tip *Bias-cut binding is easier to apply around the scalloped edges than the usual straight-cut binding.*

1. Cut the binding fabric into a square the size indicated for the quilt size you are making. Cut the square in half diagonally, creating 2 triangles.

	Square size		Square size
Baby	25" × 25"	Full	34" × 34"
Throw	29" × 29"	Queen	36" × 36"
Twin	33" × 33"	King	36" × 36"

2. Sew these triangles together as shown, using a ¼" seam allowance. Press the seam open.

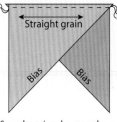

Sew the triangles together.

3. Using a ruler, mark the parallelogram created by the 2 triangles with lines spaced 2¼" apart. Cut about 5" along the first line.

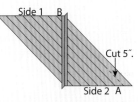

Mark the lines and begin to cut.

4. Join Side 1 and Side 2 to form a tube. The raw edge at point A will align with the raw edge at B. This will allow the first line to be offset by 1 strip width. Pin the raw edges right sides together, making sure that the drawn lines match. Sew with a ¼" seam allowance. Press the seam open. Cut along the drawn lines, creating a continuous strip.

5. Press the entire strip in half lengthwise with wrong sides together. Apply as you would straight-grain binding, mitering each inner corner.

are sewn together to create pretty flowers. Simply flip and fuse each flower to a quilt block for easy quilt-top construction.

Border fabric: *Kidz—Bright Bugs Green by Timeless Treasures, Inc.*
Other fabrics: *Courtesy of Timeless Treasures, Inc.*

Throw size shown

FABRIC REQUIREMENTS

Yardage is based on 42″ fabric width.

	Baby 38″ × 50″	Throw 50″ × 62″	Twin 62″ × 86″	Full 74″ × 86″	Queen 86″ × 86″
Number of blocks	6	12	24	30	36
Fabrics:					
Greens	2 fabrics, ½ yard *each*	4 fabrics, ½ yard *each*	4 fabrics, 1 yard *each*	5 fabrics, 1 yard *each*	6 fabrics, 1 yard *each*
Flower fabrics	3 fabrics, ½ yard *each*	6 fabrics, ½ yard *each*	4 fabrics, ¾ yard *each*	5 fabrics, ¾ yard *each*	6 fabrics, ¾ yard *each*
Yellow	⅓ yard	½ yard	¾ yard	¾ yard	¾ yard
Border and binding (if directional print)	1⅓ yards (1⅞ yards)	1⅞ yards (2½ yards)	2½ yards (3¼ yards)	2½ yards (3¼ yards)	2¾ yards (3½ yards)
Backing	2¾ yards	3⅝ yards	5⅜ yards	5⅜ yards	8 yards
Batting	46″ × 58″	58″ × 70″	70″ × 94″	82″ × 94″	94″ × 94″
Fusible interfacing (choose one):*					
C&T Appliqué Sheets	8 sheets	16 sheets	32 sheets	40 sheets	48 sheets
Pellon 911FF	2 yards	4 yards	8 yards	10 yards	12 yards

* For fusible interfacing comparisons, refer to How to Pick Your Product (page 7).

A 4″-diameter (2″–finished side) acrylic hexagon template is helpful but not necessary.

CUTTING DIRECTIONS

WOF = width of fabric; LOF = length of fabric

GREENS:

	Baby	Throw	Twin	Full	Queen
Cut 12½″ × WOF strips from *each* fabric.	1	1	2	2	2
Subcut *total* of 12½″ × 12½″ squares for block backgrounds.	6	12	24	30	36
Cut 2½″ × WOF strips from *each* fabric.	1	1	1	1	1
Use Triangle pattern (page 25) to make template and subcut *total* triangles.	18	36	72	90	108

FLOWER FABRICS:

	Baby	Throw	Twin	Full	Queen
Cut 1⅞″ × WOF strips from *each* fabric for outer edges.	4	4	8	8	8
Cut 1⅞″ × WOF strips from *each* fabric for center strips.	2	2	4	4	4

YELLOW:

	Baby	Throw	Twin	Full	Queen
Cut 2½″ × WOF strips.	1	2	3	4	4
Use Triangle template to subcut triangles.	18	36	72	90	108
Cut 1½″ × WOF strips for inner border.	4	5	7	7	8

OUTER BORDER:

	Baby	Throw	Twin	Full	Queen
If nondirectional print:					
Cut 6½" × LOF strips.	4	4	4	4	4
If directional print:					
Cut 6½" × WOF strips for top and bottom borders.	2	3	4	4	5
Cut 6½" × LOF strips for side borders.	2	2	2	2	2

BINDING:

	Baby	Throw	Twin	Full	Queen
Cut 2¼" × *remaining LOF* strips from border fabric.	4	4	4	4	4

FUSIBLE INTERFACING (CHOOSE ONE):

C&T Appliqué Sheets	Baby	Throw	Twin	Full	Queen
Cut in thirds. — Cut this many sheets in thirds along the length of each sheet.	2	4	8	10	12
Zig zag together. — Butt the long edges of a third-cut sheet and a full 8½" × 11" sheet against each other (*do not overlap*). Use a wide zigzag stitch to sew the 2 units together. Make the indicated number of units.	6	12	24	30	36

.... *or* ....

Pellon 911FF	Baby	Throw	Twin	Full	Queen
Cut 11" × 11" squares.	6	12	24	30	36

Block Construction

1. Separate the flower fabric strips into sets, each consisting of a 1⅞" center strip and 2 matching 1⅞" outer strips.

2. Sew a matching 1⅞" strip to each side of a 1⅞" center strip to make a 4⅝"-wide strip set. Press the seams toward the darker fabric. Repeat to make the required number of strip sets.

Strip sets	Baby	Throw	Twin	Full	Queen
Total strip sets	6	12	16	20	24

3. For baby and throw-size quilts, subcut 6 segments 4" wide from each strip set.

For twin-, full-, and queen-size quilts, subcut 9 segments 4" wide from each strip set.

4. Use the Hexagon pattern (page 25) to make a template. Use the Hexagon template to trim each segment into a hexagon.

Trim the 4 extending edges.   Striped hexagon

Hexagons	Baby	Throw	Twin	Full	Queen
Total hexagons*	36	72	144	180	216

* *Each flower uses 6 identical hexagons.*

5. Select 6 matching hexagons. Sew a yellow triangle to a striped side of each of 3 hexagons and a green triangle to a striped side of each of the remaining 3 hexagons.

Make 3 with yellow triangles and 3 with green triangles.

6. Sew a yellow triangle hexagon unit to each side of a green triangle hexagon unit to make a half-flower. Press the seams open.

7. Sew a green triangle hexagon unit to each side of a yellow triangle hexagon unit. Press the seams open.

8. Sew the 2 half-flowers from Steps 6 and 7 together to create a flower. Press the seam open.

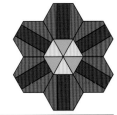

9. Repeat Steps 5–8 to make the indicated number of flowers.

Flowers	Baby	Throw	Twin	Full	Queen
Total flowers	6	12	24	30	36

Flip & Fuse

1. Pin together an 11″ × 11″ square of fusible interfacing and a pieced flower, with the glue side of the fusible interfacing toward of the right side of the fabric.

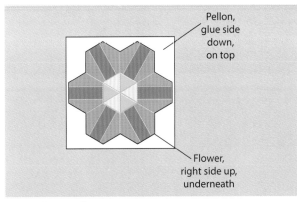

Pellon, glue side down, on top

Flower, right side up, underneath

Using Pellon interfacing

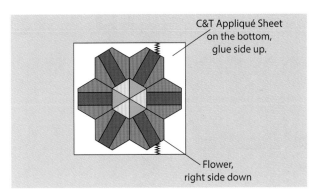

C&T Appliqué Sheet on the bottom, glue side up.

Flower, right side down

Using C&T Wash-Away Appliqué Sheet

2. Sew ¼″ in from the edge all the way around the flower as shown. If you are using Pellon fusible interfacing, it is see-through, so you can sew with the fusible side up if you like. If you are using the Wash-Away Appliqué product, sew with the pieced flower side up.

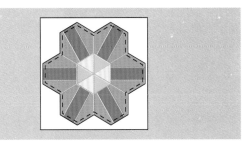

Using Pellon interfacing

3. Trim away any fusible interfacing that extends beyond the raw edge of the flower, leaving a ⅛″ seam allowance.

4. Cut a slit approximately 5″ long in the fusible interfacing, being careful not to cut the flower. Flip the unit right side out. Insert a blunt instrument inside the cut in the interfacing and gently push out the points of each flower petal. Run the blunt instrument along the edges of each piece and finger-press where the fabric and fusible interfacing meet.

5. Repeat Steps 1–4 for all the flowers.

6. Fold each 12½″ × 12½″ green background square in half vertically and horizontally and press to crease if desired. Using the creases as a guide, position each flower on a background square. Follow the manufacturer's instructions to fuse in place, using a hot iron.

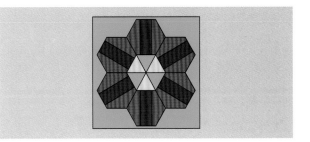

7. Using clear thread on top, sew the edges of the fused flowers to the background blocks using a blanket stitch or a zigzag stitch. Slightly lower the top tension on your machine to make sure the bobbin thread does not show on top.

Quilt Top Construction

1. Arrange the blocks in rows as shown for the selected quilt size. Sew the blocks into rows. Press the seam allowances to one side.

2. Sew the rows together to create the quilt top center. Press the seam allowances to one side.

Borders

Refer to *Summer Breeze*, Borders (page 13), to make and attach the narrow inner border and then the wider outer border to the quilt top.

Quilt assembly
Note: Your quilt may have more or less fabric variety than shown here, due to the size you chose.

Quilting Ideas

Heavier quilting in the background will help the flowers pop. I love how Laurie Vandergriff used circles in the middle strip of each hexagon to draw the viewer's eye to each flower petal. She even quilted overlapping hexagons in the final border design to echo the flower shapes.

Finishing

Layer the backing, batting, and quilt top. Baste and quilt as desired. Diagonally piece the 2¼"-wide binding strips together to form a continuous strip. Trim the seam allowances to ¼" and press to one side. Press the strip in half with wrong sides together. Attach to the quilt.

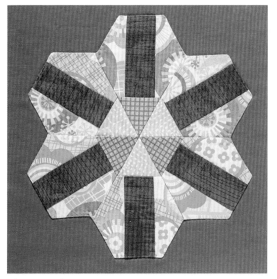

Alternate colorway

Blooming Hexagons Patterns

Seam allowances *are* included on patterns.

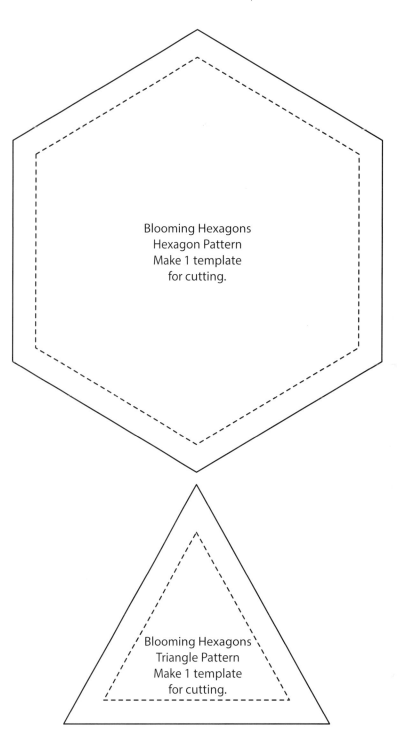

Blooming Hexagons
Hexagon Pattern
Make 1 template
for cutting.

Blooming Hexagons
Triangle Pattern
Make 1 template
for cutting.

Circle Burst

Finished block: 12″ × 12″

Finished quilt: Throw 50″ × 62″ (size shown)

This quilt is easier than it looks. Melon shapes cut from pieced rectangles are fused onto Pinwheel blocks to create the circular look.

Border fabric: *Fun—Hedgehogs Black by Timeless Treasures, Inc.*
Other fabrics: *Courtesy of Timeless Treasures, Inc.*

FABRIC REQUIREMENTS Yardage is based on 42″ fabric width.

	Baby 38″ × 50″	Throw 50″ × 62″	Twin 62″ × 86″	Full 74″ × 86″	Queen 86″ × 86″
Number of blocks	6	12	24	30	36
Fabrics:					
Yellow	½ yard	1 yard	1¾ yards	2¼ yards	2¾ yards
Green	½ yard	1 yard	1¾ yards	2¼ yards	2¾ yards
Dark blue	¼ yard	½ yard	⅞ yard	1 yard	1¼ yards
Orange	¼ yard	½ yard	⅞ yard	1 yard	1¼ yards
Light blue	¼ yard	½ yard	⅞ yard	1 yard	1¼ yards
Red	¼ yard	½ yard	⅞ yard	1 yard	1¼ yards
Inner border	¼ yard	⅓ yard	⅜ yard	⅜ yard	⅜ yard
Outer border *(if directional print)*	1¼ yards *(1⅝ yards)*	1⅝ yards *(2¼ yards)*	2¼ yards *(3 yards)*	2¼ yards *(3 yards)*	2⅝ yards *(3½ yards)*
Backing	2¾ yards	3⅝ yards	5⅜ yards	5⅜ yards	8 yards
Binding	⅜ yard	½ yard	⅝ yard	⅝ yard	⅝ yard
Batting	46″ × 58″	58″ × 70″	70″ × 94″	82″ × 94″	94″ × 94″
Fusible interfacing (choose one):*					
C&T Appliqué Sheets	12 sheets	24 sheets	48 sheets	60 sheets	72 sheets
Pellon 911FF	1½ yards	2¾ yards	5 yards	6¼ yards	7½ yards

* *For fusible interfacing comparisons, refer to How to Pick Your Product (page 7).*

CUTTING DIRECTIONS *WOF = width of fabric; LOF = length of fabric*

YELLOW AND GREEN:

	Baby	Throw	Twin	Full	Queen
Cut 6⅞″ × WOF strips from *each* fabric.	2	4	8	10	12
Subcut 6⅞″ × 6⅞″ squares from *each* fabric.	12	24	48	60	72
Subcut each 6⅞″ × 6⅞″ square once diagonally to create indicated number of triangles from *each* fabric.	24	48	96	120	144

DARK BLUE, ORANGE, LIGHT BLUE, AND RED:

	Baby	Throw	Twin	Full	Queen
Cut 2″ × WOF strips from *each* fabric.	3	6	12	15	18

INNER BORDER:

	Baby	Throw	Twin	Full	Queen
Cut 1½″ × WOF strips.	4	5	7	7	8

	Baby	Throw	Twin	Full	Queen
If nondirectional print:					
Cut 6½″ × LOF strips.	4	4	4	4	4
If directional print:					
Cut 6½″ × WOF strips.	2	3	4	4	5
Cut 6½″ × remaining LOF strips.	2	2	2	2	2

BINDING:

Note: If you would like to use the remaining border fabric for the binding, refer to Blooming Hexagons, Binding (page 22), for cutting instructions.

	Baby	Throw	Twin	Full	Queen
Cut 2¼″ × WOF strips.	5	6	8	9	9

FUSIBLE INTERFACING (CHOOSE ONE):

• C&T Wash-Away Appliqué Sheets

Follow the manufacturer's instructions to print the indicated number of Circle Burst patterns (page 79) onto the *nonfusible* side of 8½″ × 11″ sheets of interfacing, using your inkjet printer.

Note: If using C&T Wash-Away Appliqué Roll, follow the instructions for Pellon interfacing (below).

C&T Appliqué Sheets	Baby	Throw	Twin	Full	Queen
Number of copies	12	24	48	60	72

.... *or* ....

• Pellon 911FF Fusible Featherweight interfacing

Cut the interfacing into the indicated sizes and quantities of pieces. Trace 1 shape onto the *nonfusible* side of each corresponding interfacing piece.

Pellon 911FF	Baby	Throw	Twin	Full	Queen
Melons: 3½″ × 9½″	24	48	96	120	144

Melon

Block Construction

1. Sew a yellow 6⅞″ half-square triangle to a green 6⅞″ half-square triangle to yield a half-square triangle (HST) unit. Press the seam toward the green triangle. Repeat to make the required number of HST units.

	Baby	Throw	Twin	Full	Queen
Half-square triangle units	24	48	96	120	144

2. Sew 2 HST units from Step 1 together to form a half-block, paying attention to the color placement. Press the seam to one side. Repeat to make the required number of half-blocks.

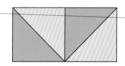

	Baby	Throw	Twin	Full	Queen
Half-blocks	12	24	48	60	72

3. Sew 2 half-blocks from Step 2 together as shown to create a whole block. Press the seam open. Repeat to make the required number of whole blocks.

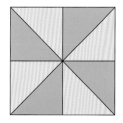

	Baby	Throw	Twin	Full	Queen
Whole blocks	6	12	24	30	36

4. Sew a 2″-wide red strip and a 2″-wide light blue strip together to make a strip set. Press the seam to one side. Subcut into 8 rectangles 3½″ × 5″. Repeat to make the required number of rectangles.

Strip sets and rectangles	Baby	Throw	Twin	Full	Queen
Red / light blue strip sets	3	6	12	15	18
Red / light blue rectangles	24	48	96	120	144

5. Repeat Step 4 with the 2″-wide orange and dark blue strips.

Strip sets and rectangles	Baby	Throw	Twin	Full	Queen
Orange / dark blue strip sets	3	6	12	15	18
Orange / dark blue rectangles	24	48	96	120	144

6. Sew a red / light blue rectangle to an orange / dark blue rectangle to create a 3½″ × 9½″ rectangle as shown. Press the seam to one side. Repeat to make the required number of rectangles. Make sure the fabrics are in the same position for all units.

	Baby	Throw	Twin	Full	Queen
Pieced rectangles	24	48	96	120	144

Flip & Fuse

For detailed instructions on this method, refer to How Flip & Fuse Works (page 5).

1. If you are using the C&T Wash-Away Appliqué Sheets, cut apart the Melon patterns. Leave at least ⅛″ beyond the drawn lines.

2. Place the fusible interfacing on a pieced rectangle so that the fusible side of the interfacing is facing the right side of the pieced rectangle.

Fabric right side up

Interfacing glue side down

3. Sew on the line.

4. Trim the excess fabric and fusible interfacing ⅛″ beyond the stitched line.

5. Cut a slit measuring approximately 4″ in the interfacing (making sure to not cut the fabric!).

Trim fabric and interfacing ⅛″ beyond stitching.

Cut a slit in the interfacing only.

6. Flip the unit right side out. Insert a blunt instrument inside the cut in the interfacing and gently push out the points of the unit. Run the blunt instrument along the edges of the piece and finger-press the edges where the fabric and fusible interfacing meet.

7. Repeat Steps 2–6 for all the pieced-rectangle melons.

8. Place 4 units from Step 6 on a block as shown. Make sure the tips of the melon units are positioned ¼″ in from the raw edge of the block so they are not sewn into a seam. Also, pay attention to the color placement of the melon pieces. Follow the manufacturer's instructions to fuse the melon units to the block, using a hot iron.

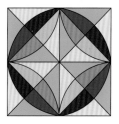

9. Using clear thread on top, sew the edge of each fused unit to the background block using a blanket stitch or a zigzag stitch. Slightly lower the top tension on your machine to make sure the bobbin thread does not show on top.

10. Repeat Steps 8 and 9 to appliqué all the blocks.

Quilt Top Construction

1. Arrange the blocks in rows as shown for the selected quilt size. Sew the blocks into rows. Press the seams to one side.

2. Sew the rows together to create the quilt top center. Press the seams to one side.

Borders

Refer to *Summer Breeze*, Borders (page 13), to make and attach the narrow inner border and then the wider outer border to the quilt top.

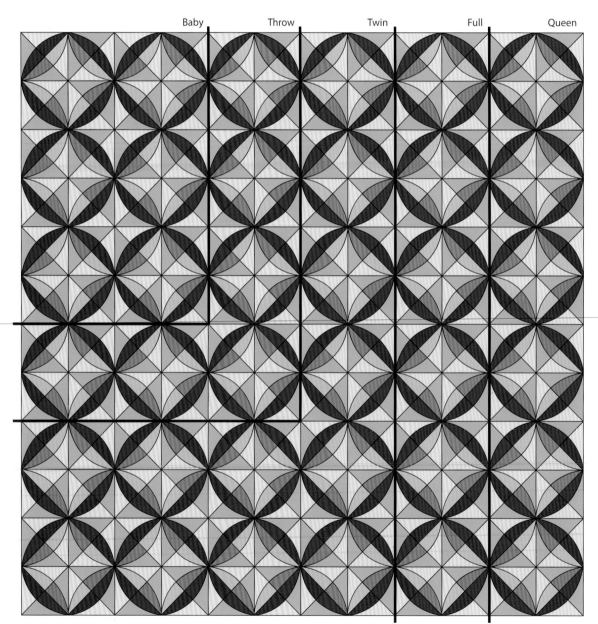

Quilt assembly

Quilting Ideas

Laurie Vandergriff quilted melons and circles in the outside border to echo the design in the middle of the quilt. She also stitched straight lines to accentuate the pinwheels and incorporated pretty swirls on pieced melon units for the blocks.

Finishing

Layer the backing, batting, and quilt top. Baste and quilt as desired. Diagonally piece the 2¼"-wide binding strips together to form a continuous strip. Trim the seam allowances to ¼" and press to one side. Press the strip in half with wrong sides together. Attach to the quilt.

Alternate colorway

The Watering Hole

Finished block: 6″ × 9″

Finished quilt: Twin 74″ × 86″ (size shown)

This quilt would also look great as a two-color quilt. Just make sure there is good value contrast between the one light fabric and the one dark fabric.

Border fabric: *Cork Cinnabar by Hoffman Fabrics*
Other fabrics: *Courtesy of Hoffman Fabrics*

FABRIC REQUIREMENTS

Yardage is based on 42" fabric width. An assortment of dark and light fabrics adds interest to this quilt. Please refer to the suggested number of fabrics and associated yardage for *each*.

	Baby 38" × 50"	Throw 50" × 68"	Twin 74" × 86"	Full 86" × 86"	Queen 98" × 104"	King 110" × 104"
Number of blocks	16	36	80	96	140	160
Fabrics:						
Dark fabrics	4 fabrics, ⅝ yard *each*	5 fabrics, ⅝ yard *each*	5 fabrics, 1¼ yards *each*	6 fabrics, 1¼ yards *each*	9 fabrics, 1¼ yards *each*	10 fabrics, 1¼ yards *each*
Light fabrics	4 fabrics, ⅝ yard *each*	5 fabrics, ⅝ yard *each*	5 fabrics, 1¼ yards *each*	6 fabrics, 1¼ yards *each*	9 fabrics, 1¼ yards *each*	10 fabrics, 1¼ yards *each*
Inner border	¼ yard	¼ yard	⅜ yard	½ yard	½ yard	⅝ yard
Outer border and binding (if directional print)	1⅓ yards (2 yards)	2 yards (2¾ yards)	2½ yards (3¼ yards)	2¾ yards (3½ yards)	3⅛ yards (4⅛ yards)	3½ yards (4¾ yards)
Backing	2¾ yards	3½ yards	5⅜ yards	8 yards	9 yards	9¼ yards
Batting	46" × 58"	58" × 76"	82" × 94"	94" × 94"	106" × 112"	118" × 112"
Fusible interfacing (choose one):*						
C&T Appliqué Sheets	32 sheets	72 sheets	160 sheets	192 sheets	280 sheets	320 sheets
Pellon 911FF	2½ yards	5 yards	10½ yards	12 yards	18 yards	21 yards

* For fusible interfacing comparisons, refer to How to Pick Your Product (page 7).

CUTTING DIRECTIONS

WOF = width of fabric; LOF = length of fabric

LIGHT AND DARK FABRICS:

	Baby	Throw	Twin	Full	Queen	King
Cut 6½" × WOF strips from *each* fabric.	1	1	2	2	2	2
Subcut *total* of 6½" × 9½" rectangles.	8 light, 8 dark	18 light, 18 dark	40 light, 40 dark	48 light, 48 dark	70 light, 70 dark	80 light, 80 dark
Cut 5¾" × WOF strips from *each* fabric.	1	1	2	2	2	2
Subcut *total* of 5¾" × 4¼" rectangles.	16 light, 16 dark	36 light, 36 dark	80 light, 80 dark	96 light, 96 dark	140 light, 140 dark	160 light, 160 dark
Cut 3¼" × WOF strips from *each* fabric.	1	1	2	2	2	2
Subcut *total* of 3¼" × 4¾" rectangles.	16 light, 16 dark	36 light, 36 dark	80 light, 80 dark	96 light, 96 dark	140 light, 140 dark	160 light, 160 dark

DARK FINAL BORDER:

	Baby	Throw	Twin	Full	Queen	King
If nondirectional print:						
Cut 6½" × LOF strips.	4	4	4	4	4	4
If directional print:						
Cut 6½" × WOF strips for top and bottom borders.	2	3	4	5	6	7
Cut 6½" × remaining LOF strips for side borders.	2	2	2	2	2	2

INNER BORDER:

	Baby	Throw	Twin	Full	Queen	King
Cut 1½" × WOF strips.	4	5	7	8	9	10

BINDING:

	Baby	Throw	Twin	Full	Queen	King
Cut 2¼" × remaining LOF strips of border fabric.	4	4	4	4	4	4

FUSIBLE INTERFACING (CHOOSE ONE):

- **C&T Wash-Away Appliqué Sheets**

  Follow the manufacturer's instructions to print the indicated number of Watering Hole pattern sheets (pages 80 and 81) onto the *nonfusible* side of 8½" × 11" sheets of interfacing, using your inkjet printer.

  Note: If using C&T Wash-Away Appliqué Roll, follow the instructions for Pellon interfacing (below).

C&T Appliqué Sheets	Baby	Throw	Twin	Full	Queen	King
Copies of Sheet 1	16	36	80	96	140	160
Copies of Sheet 2	16	36	80	96	140	160

or

- **Pellon 911FF Fusible Featherweight interfacing**   Cut the interfacing into the indicated sizes and quantities of pieces. Trace 1 shape onto the *nonfusible* side of each corresponding interfacing piece.

Pellon 911FF	Baby	Throw	Twin	Full	Queen	King
Large quarter-oval: 4¼" × 5¾"	32 (16 and 16R*)	72 (36 and 36R)	160 (80 and 80R)	192 (96 and 96R)	280 (140 and 140R)	320 (160 and 160R)
Small quarter-oval: 3¼" × 4¾"	32 (16 and 16R)	72 (36 and 36R)	160 (80 and 80R)	192 (96 and 96R)	280 (140 and 140R)	320 (160 and 160R)

* R = reversed

Small quarter-oval   Small reversed quarter-oval   Large quarter-oval   Large reversed quarter-oval

Flip & Fuse

For detailed instructions on this method, refer to How Flip & Fuse Works (page 5).

1. If you are using the C&T Wash-Away Appliqué Sheets, cut apart the Large Quarter-Oval and Small Quarter-Oval patterns.

2. Align the straight edges of a large quarter-oval interfacing piece on a 4¼″ × 5¾″ rectangle of fabric as shown, with the glue side of the fusible interfacing touching the right side of the fabric.

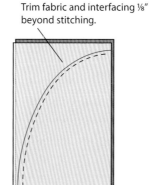

Trim fabric and interfacing ⅛″ beyond stitching.

3. Sew on the curved line.

4. Repeat Step 2 to sew a small quarter-oval interfacing piece to a 3¼″ × 4¾″ rectangle.

5. Trim the excess fabric and interfacing to a ⅛″ seam allowance.

6. Flip the units right side out. Use a blunt instrument to gently push out the edges along the seam and finger-press.

7. Repeat Steps 2–6 for all the appliqué pieces. Keep the same shapes grouped together.

R = reversed shapes

Oval units	Baby	Throw	Twin	Full	Queen	King
Dark large quarter-ovals	16 (8 and 8R*)	36 (16 and 20R)	80 (40 and 40R)	96 (48 and 48R)	140 (68 and 72R)	160 (80 and 80R)
Dark small quarter-ovals	16 (8 and 8R)	36 (20 and 16R)	80 (40 and 40R)	96 (48 and 48R)	140 (72 and 68R)	160 (80 and 80R)
Light large quarter-ovals	16 (8 and 8R)	36 (20 and 16R)	80 (40 and 40R)	96 (48 and 48R)	140 (72 and 68R)	160 (80 and 80R)
Light small quarter-ovals	16 (8 and 8R)	36 (16 and 20R)	80 (40 and 40R)	96 (48 and 48R)	140 (68 and 72R)	160 (80 and 80R)

* R = reversed

Block Construction

1. To make a light block, position dark large quarter-ovals in the upper right and lower left corners of a light 6½″ × 9½″ rectangle as shown. Follow the manufacturer's instructions to fuse in place.

2. Position light small quarter-ovals on top of the dark large quarter-ovals fused to the background in Step 1. Fuse in place.

Light block

3. To make a reversed light block, position dark reversed large quarter-ovals in the upper left and lower right corners of a light 6½″ × 9½″ rectangle as shown. Fuse in place.

4. Position light small reversed quarter-ovals on top of the dark large reversed quarter-ovals from Step 3. Fuse in place.

Reversed light block

5. Repeat Steps 1–4 to make the required number of light and reversed light blocks.

Light and reversed light blocks	Baby	Throw	Twin	Full	Queen	King
Light blocks	4	8	20	24	34	40
Reversed light blocks	4	10	20	24	36	40

6. To make a dark block, position light large quarter-ovals in the upper right and lower left corners of a dark 6½" × 9½" rectangle as shown. Fuse in place.

7. Position dark small quarter-ovals on top of the light large quarter-ovals fused to the background in Step 6. Fuse in place.

Dark block

8. To make a reversed dark block, position light large reversed quarter-ovals in the upper left and lower right corners of a dark 6½" × 9½" rectangle as shown. Fuse in place.

9. Position dark small reversed quarter-ovals on the light large reversed quarter-ovals from Step 8. Fuse in place.

Reversed dark block

10. Repeat Steps 6–9 to make the required number of dark and reversed dark blocks.

Dark and reversed dark blocks	Baby	Throw	Twin	Full	Queen	King
Dark blocks	4	10	20	24	36	40
Reversed dark blocks	4	8	20	24	34	40

11. Using clear thread on top, sew the curved edges of the fused pieces to the background blocks using a blanket stitch or a zigzag stitch. Slightly lower the top tension on your machine to make sure the bobbin thread does not show on top.

Quilt Top Construction

1. Arrange the blocks as shown in the quilt assembly diagram (at right) for the selected quilt size. Pay careful attention to the placement of the blocks to create the overall pattern. All the regular blocks (light and dark) are in the upper right and lower left quadrants. All the reversed blocks (light and dark) are in the upper left and lower right quadrants.

2. Sew the blocks together to form rows. Press the seams open.

3. Sew the rows together to create the quilt top center. Press the seams open.

Reversed block

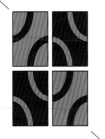

Reversed block

Quilt assembly
Note: Your quilt may have more fabric variety than shown here, due to the size you chose.

Bor~~ders~~

Refer ~~...~~ the narrow inner
borde~~...~~

Fir~~...~~

Layer ~~...~~ed. Diagonally
piece ~~...~~ strip. Trim the
seam ~~...~~alf with wrong
sides ~~...~~

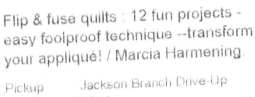

Alternate colorway

Baby size, alternate colorway

Border fabric: *Dilly Dally by Me and My Sister Designs for Moda*

Splash

Finished block: 6″ × 12″

Finished quilt: Throw 62″ × 74″ (size shown)

Difficulty: Level 1

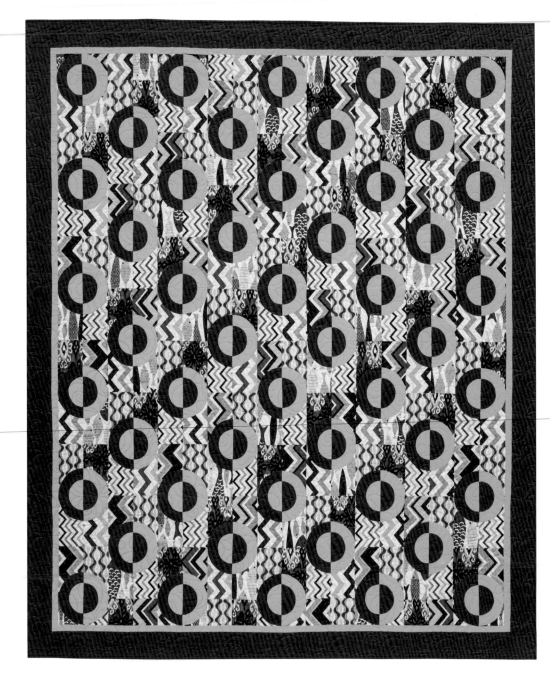

Solid fabrics make the circles stand out from the textured background.

....

Fabrics: *Courtesy of Michael Miller Fabrics*

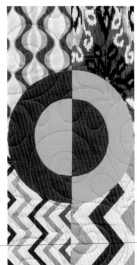

FABRIC REQUIREMENTS

An assortment of prints are used for the background for added interest. Please refer to the suggested number of fabrics and associated yardage for *each*.

Yardage is based on 42″ fabric width.

	Baby 38″ × 50″	Throw 62″ × 74″	Twin 74″ × 86″	Full 86″ × 86″	Queen 98″ × 98″	King 110″ × 110″
Number of blocks	18 whole, 4 half	50 whole, 8 half	72 whole, 10 half	85 whole, 12 half	113 whole, 14 half	145 whole, 16 half
Fabrics:						
Background prints	5 fabrics, ½ yard *each*	6 fabrics, ¾ yard *each*	6 fabrics, 1 yard *each*	7 fabrics, 1 yard *each*	8 fabrics, 1¼ yards *each*	8 fabrics, 1½ yards *each*
Aqua solid (appliqué and inner border)	¾ yard	1¾ yards	2⅓ yards	2¾ yards	3½ yards	4½ yards
Dark blue solid (appliqué, outer border, and binding)	1½ yards	2¾ yards	3⅓ yards	3¾ yards	4¾ yards	5⅝ yards
Backing	2¾ yards	4 yards	5⅜ yards	8 yards	9 yards	10 yards
Batting	46″ × 58″	70″ × 82″	82″ × 94″	94″ × 94″	106″ × 106″	118″ × 118″
Fusible interfacing (choose one):*						
C&T Appliqué Sheets	18 sheets	50 sheets	72 sheets	85 sheets	113 sheets	145 sheets
Pellon 911FF	1¾ yards	4½ yards	6½ yards	7½ yards	10 yards	12½ yards

* For fusible interfacing comparisons, refer to How to Pick Your Product (page 7)

CUTTING DIRECTIONS   *WOF = width of fabric; LOF = length of fabric*

BACKGROUND PRINTS:

	Baby	Throw	Twin	Full	Queen	King
Cut 3½″ × WOF strips from *each* background print.	3	6	9	9	10	13
Subcut *total* of 3½″ × 6½″ rectangles.	80	216	308	364	480	612

DARK BLUE SOLID:

	Baby	Throw	Twin	Full	Queen	King
Cut 3½″ × WOF strips for large appliqués and outer border.	8	16	20	24	29	36
Cut 2¼″ × WOF strips for small appliqués and binding.	7	13	17	18	23	27

AQUA SOLID:

	Baby	Throw	Twin	Full	Queen	King
Cut 3½″ × WOF strips for large appliqués.	3	9	12	15	19	25
Cut 2¼″ × WOF strips for small appliqués.	2	5	8	9	12	15
Cut 1½″ × WOF strips for inner border.	4	7	8	8	10	11

· C&T Wash-Away Appliqué Sheets

Follow the manufacturer's instructions to print the indicated number of Splash pattern sheets (page 82) onto the *nonfusible* side of 8½" × 11" sheets of interfacing, using your inkjet printer.

Note: If using C&T Wash-Away Appliqué Roll, follow the instructions for Pellon interfacing (at right).

C&T Appliqué Sheets	Baby	Throw	Twin	Full	Queen	King
Number of copies	18	50	72	85	113	145

···················· *or* ····················

· Pellon 911FF Fusible Featherweight interfacing

Cut the interfacing into the indicated sizes and quantities of pieces. Trace 1 shape (page 82) onto the *nonfusible* side of each corresponding interfacing piece. Trace the dotted line through the centers as a guide for positioning later.

Pellon 911FF	Baby	Throw	Twin	Full	Queen	King
Large circles: 6½" × 6½"	18	50	72	85	113	145
Small circles: 4" × 4"	18	50	72	85	113	145

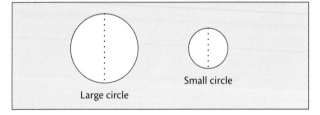

Large circle   Small circle

Flip & Fuse

For detailed instructions on this method, refer to How Flip & Fuse Works (page 5).

1. Sew a 3½"-wide strip of aqua solid fabric and a 3½"-wide strip of dark blue solid fabric together. Press the seam toward the dark blue fabric. Repeat to make the required number of strip sets.

	Baby	Throw	Twin	Full	Queen	King
Large strip sets	3	9	12	15	19	25

2. Subcut each large strip set into 6 squares 6½" × 6½".

3. Sew a 2¼"-wide strip of aqua solid fabric and a 2¼"-wide strip of dark blue solid fabric together. Press the seam toward the dark blue solid fabric. Repeat to make the required number of strip sets.

4. Subcut each small strip set into 10 squares 4" × 4".

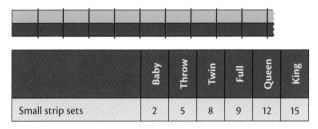

	Baby	Throw	Twin	Full	Queen	King
Small strip sets	2	5	8	9	12	15

5. If you are using C&T Wash-Away Appliqué Sheets, cut apart the Circle patterns. Leave at least ⅛" beyond the solid lines.

6. Center each large circle of fusible interfacing on a pieced 6½" × 6½" aqua solid / dark blue solid square, aligning the center guideline with the seamline. Make sure the fusible side of the interfacing is facing the right side of the fabric.

Fabric right side up

Interfacing glue side down

7. Sew on the solid lines.

8. Trim the excess fabric and fusible interfacing ⅛″ beyond the sewn lines.

9. Cut a slit measuring approximately 3″ in the interfacing of each piece (making sure not to cut the fabric!).

Trim fabric and interfacing ⅛″ beyond stitching.

Cut a slit in the interfacing only.

10. Flip each unit right side out. Insert a blunt instrument inside the cut in the interfacing and gently push around the edges of each unit where the fabric and fusible interfacing meet.

11. Repeat Steps 6–10 using the small circles of fusible interfacing on pieced 4″ × 4″ aqua / dark blue squares.

Circle units	Baby	Throw	Twin	Full	Queen	King
Large circles	18	50	72	85	113	145
Small circles	18	50	72	85	113	145

Block Construction

1. Sew 2 background print 3½″ × 6½″ rectangles together to form a half-block. Repeat to make the required number of half-blocks.

	Baby	Throw	Twin	Full	Queen	King
Half-blocks	40	108	154	182	240	306

2. Sew 2 half-blocks together to form a block that measures 6½″ × 12½″ unfinished. Follow the chart to make the indicated number of blocks. Set aside the remaining half-blocks.

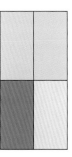

Blocks	Baby	Throw	Twin	Full	Queen	King
Full blocks	18	50	72	85	113	145
Remaining half-blocks	4	8	10	12	14	16

3. Center a large circle unit and a small circle unit on a block as shown, aligning the center seams. Make sure the dark blue side of the large circle unit is on the left side and the dark blue side of the small circle unit is on the right side as shown. The circles are positioned ¼″ in from the side raw edges of the block. (The seam allowance is not shown in the diagram.) Use a hot iron to fuse in place.

4. Using clear thread on top, sew the edge of each fused piece to the background block using a blanket stitch or a zigzag stitch. Slightly lower the top tension on your machine to make sure the bobbin thread does not show on top.

5. Repeat Steps 3 and 4 for all the blocks.

Quilt Top Construction

1. Lay out the blocks and half-blocks in columns as shown in the quilt assembly diagram for the selected quilt size. The odd-numbered rows will contain all whole blocks, while the even-numbered rows will have half-blocks on the top and the bottom. Sew the blocks together to form columns. Press the seams to one side.

2. Sew the columns together to form the quilt top center. Press the seams to one side.

3. Trim the top and bottom of the quilt top center ¼" beyond the top and bottom circles as shown in the quilt assembly diagram.

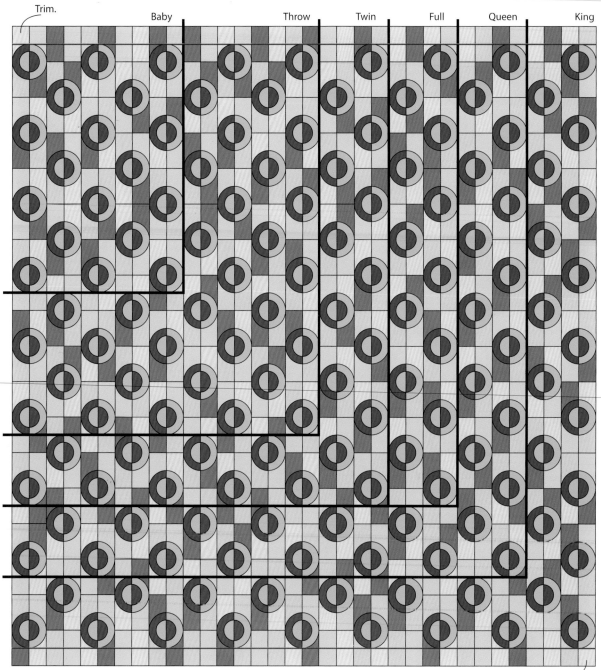

Quilt assembly

Note: Your quilt may have more or less fabric variety than shown here, due to the size you chose.

Borders

Refer to *Summer Breeze*, Borders (page 13), to make and attach the narrow inner border and then the wider outer border to the quilt top.

Finishing

Layer the backing, batting, and quilt top. Baste and quilt as desired. Diagonally piece the 2¼"-wide dark blue binding strips together to form a continuous strip. Trim the seam allowances to ¼" and press to one side. Press the strip in half with wrong sides together. Attach to the quilt.

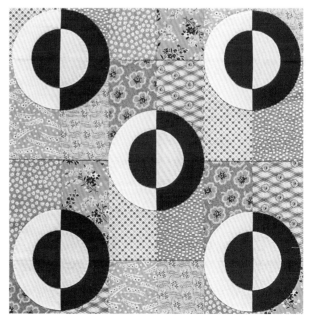

Alternate colorway

Wagon Wheels

Difficulty: Level 1

Finished block: 16″ × 16″

Finished quilt: Throw 61½″ × 77½″ (size shown)

Pie wedges and circles are all it takes to create a wagon wheel. What a fantastic scrappy quilt opportunity!

Border fabric: *Aurora Borealis by Michael Miller Fabrics;*
Other fabrics: *Courtesy of Michael Miller Fabrics*

FABRIC REQUIREMENTS

Yardage is based on 42″ fabric width. An assortment of fabrics are used for the wheels. Please refer to the suggested number of fabrics and associated yardage for *each*.

	Wall 45½″ × 45½″	Baby 45½″ × 61½″	Throw 61½″ × 77½″	Twin/Full 77½″ × 93½″	Queen 93½″ × 93½″	King 109½″ × 109½″
Number of blocks	4	6	12	20	25	36
Fabrics:						
Background	1¼ yards	1½ yards	3 yards	5 yards	6½ yards	8¾ yards
Wheel fabrics	5 fabrics, ¼ yard *each*	7 fabrics, ¼ yard *each*	7 fabrics, ½ yard *each*	11 fabrics, ½ yard *each*	10 fabrics, ¾ yard *each*	12 fabrics, ⅞ yard *each*
Circles / inner border	⅓ yard	⅜ yard	½ yard	¾ yard	¾ yard	1 yard
Border and binding *(if directional print)*	1½ yards (1¾ yards)	1¾ yards (2½ yards)	2 yards (3 yards)	2½ yards (3½ yards)	3 yards (3¾ yards)	3¼ yards (4½ yards)
Backing	3¼ yards	3½ yards	5 yards	5⅞ yards	8⅝ yards	10 yards
Batting	54″ × 54″	54″ × 70″	70″ × 86″	86″ × 102″	102″ × 102″	118″ × 118″
Fusible interfacing (choose one):*						
C&T Appliqué Sheets	11 sheets	16 sheets	32 sheets	52 sheets	65 sheets	94 sheets
Pellon 911FF	2½ yards	3½ yards	6½ yards	10 yards	12½ yards	18 yards

* For fusible interfacing comparisons, refer to How to Pick Your Product (page 7).

CUTTING DIRECTIONS

WOF = width of fabric; LOF = length of fabric

BACKGROUND:

	Wall	Baby	Throw	Twin/Full	Queen	King
Cut 16½″ × WOF strips.	2	3	6	10	13	18
Subcut 16½″ × 16½″ squares.	4	6	12	20	25	36

WHEEL FABRICS:

	Wall	Baby	Throw	Twin/Full	Queen	King
Cut 6¾″ × WOF strips from *each* fabric.	1	1	2	2	3	4
Subcut *total* of 6¾″ × 3¾″ rectangles.	48	72	144	240	300	432

INNER BORDER AND APPLIQUÉ CIRCLES:

	Wall	Baby	Throw	Twin/Full	Queen	King
Cut 3½″ × WOF strips.	1	1	1	2	3	3
Subcut 3½″ × 3½″ squares.	4	6	12	20	25	36
Cut 1¼″ × WOF strips for inner border.	4	5	6	8	9	10

OUTER BORDER:

	Wall	Baby	Throw	Twin/Full	Queen	King
If nondirectional print:						
Cut 6½″ × LOF strips.	4	4	4	4	4	4
If directional print:						
Cut 6½″ × WOF strips for top and bottom borders.	3	3	4	5	6	6
Cut 6½″ × *remaining LOF* strips for side borders.	2	2	2	2	2	2

BINDING:

Cut 2¼″ × remaining LOF strips.	Wall	Baby	Throw	Twin/Full	Queen	King
	6	5	5	5	5	5

FUSIBLE INTERFACING (CHOOSE ONE):

- **C&T Wash-Away Appliqué Sheets**   Follow the manufacturer's instructions to print the indicated number of Wagon Wheels pattern sheets (pages 83 and 84) onto the *nonfusible* side of 8½″ × 11″ sheets of interfacing, using your inkjet printer.

  Note: If using C&T Wash-Away Appliqué Roll, follow the instructions for Pellon interfacing (below).

C&T Appliqué Sheets	Wall	Baby	Throw	Twin/Full	Queen	King
Sheet 1	7	10	20	32	40	58
Sheet 2	4	6	12	20	25	36

.... *or* ....

- **Pellon 911FF Fusible Featherweight interfacing**
  Cut the interfacing into the indicated sizes and quantities of pieces. Trace 1 shape (pages 83 and 84) onto the *nonfusible* side of each corresponding interfacing piece.

Pellon 911FF	Wall	Baby	Throw	Twin/Full	Queen	King
Wedges: 3¾″ × 6¾″	48	72	144	240	300	432
Circles: 3½″ × 3½″	4	6	12	20	25	36

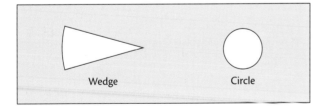

Wedge   Circle

Flip & Fuse

For detailed instructions on this method, refer to How Flip & Fuse Works (page 5).

1. If you are using the C&T Wash-Away Appliqué Sheets, cut apart the Wedge and Circle patterns. Leave at least ⅛″ beyond the drawn lines.

2. Place each of the wedge fusible interfacing pieces on a 3¾″ × 6¾″ rectangle of wheel fabric so the fusible side of the interfacing is facing the right side of the fabric.

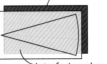

Fabric right side up

Interfacing glue side down

3. Sew on the line.

4. Trim the excess fabric and fusible interfacing ⅛″ beyond the sewn lines.

5. Cut a slit in the interfacing of each piece (making sure not to cut the fabric!).

Trim fabric and interfacing ⅛″ beyond stitching.

Cut a slit in the interfacing only.

6. Flip the units right side out. Insert a blunt instrument inside the cut in the interfacing and gently push out the points and edges of each unit. Run the blunt instrument along the edges of each piece and finger-press the edges where the fabric and fusible interfacing meet. Set the prepared wedges aside until the blocks are constructed.

7. Repeat Steps 2–6 using the circle fusible interfacing pieces on 3½″ × 3½″ squares of circle fabric to make the wheel centers.

Block Construction

1. Fold a background square in half both vertically and horizontally and press to crease. Select 12 wagon wheel units and 1 wheel center piece. Position the wedges on the square in a wheel shape, first centering 1 wedge on each crease about ¾" from the center of the block and then filling in with the remaining 8 wedges; then add the circle on top. Use a hot iron to fuse in place. Repeat to make the required number of blocks.

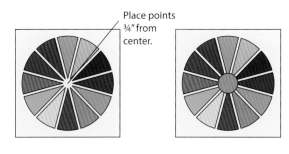

Place points ¾" from center.

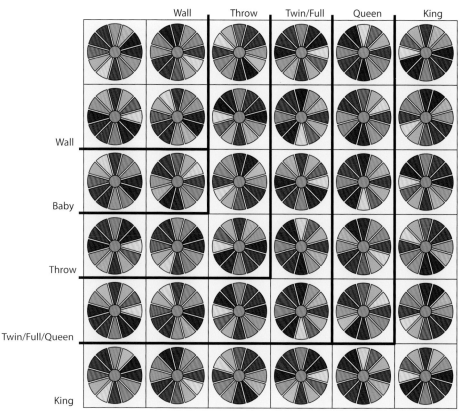

	Wall	Baby	Throw	Twin/Full	Queen	King
Blocks	4	6	12	20	25	36

2. Using clear thread on top, sew the edges of the fused pieces to the background blocks using a blanket stitch or a zigzag stitch. Slightly lower the top tension on your machine to make sure the bobbin thread does not show on top.

Quilt Top Center Construction

1. Arrange the blocks as shown for the selected quilt size. Sew the blocks into rows. Press the seams to one side.

2. Sew the rows together to create the quilt top center. Press the seams to one side.

Borders

Refer to *Summer Breeze*, Borders (page 13), to make and attach the narrow inner border and then the wider outer border to the quilt top.

Quilt assembly
Note: Your quilt may have more or less fabric variety than shown here, due to the size you chose.

Finishing

Layer the backing, batting, and quilt top. Baste and quilt as desired. Diagonally piece the 2¼"-wide binding strips together to form a continuous strip. Trim the seam allowances to ¼" and press to one side. Press the strip in half with wrong sides together. Attach to the quilt.

Quilting Ideas

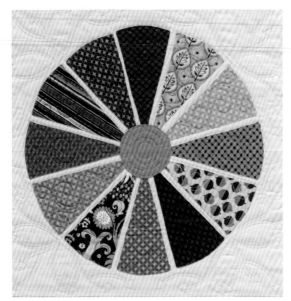

Alternate colorway

Laurie Vandergriff quilted beautiful swirls in each of the wheel wedge pieces. She used a geometric circle design in the center of the wheel. Check out her fun whimsical arrow designs for the background.

Wallhanging version; longarm quilting by Laurie Vandergriff

Hoppy

Finished blocks: 5″ × 5″

Finished quilt: 45″ × 55″

Difficulty:
Level 3

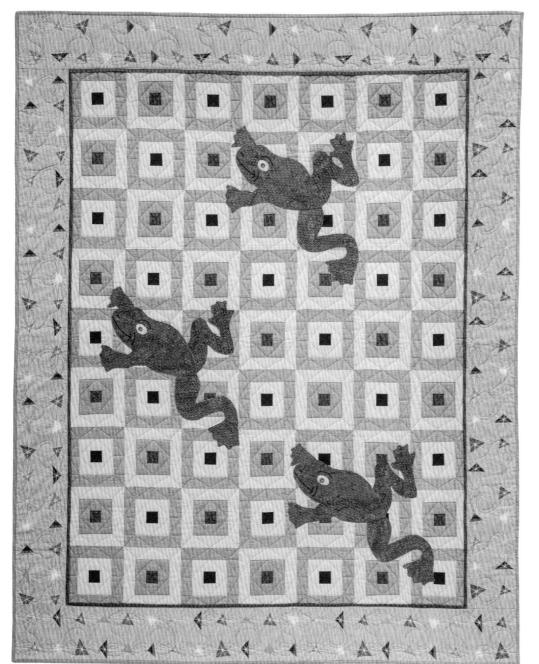

Small frog legs can be challenging to flip right side out. Just take a little time and use some finesse and you'll have these frogs hopping onto your quilt in no time.

Fabrics: *Mod Century fabrics by Jenn Ski courtesy of Moda*

FABRIC REQUIREMENTS

Yardage is based on 42″ fabric width.

CREAM: 1½ yards

GREEN: 1½ yards

RED: ⅛ yard

ORANGE: ¼ yard

FROG GREEN: ¾ yard

BORDER: 1½ yards

BINDING: ½ yard

BACKING: 3⅛ yards

BATTING: 53″ × 63″

FUSIBLE INTERFACING: C&T Wash-Away Appliqué Sheets (6 sheets) *or* Pellon 911FF Fusible Featherweight interfacing (2 yards)

Other supplies:

WATER-SOLUBLE PEN

DARK GREEN PERMANENT FABRIC PEN

DARK GREEN THREAD FOR SATIN STITCH MACHINE EMBROIDERY

CUTTING DIRECTIONS

WOF = width of fabric; LOF = length of fabric

CREAM:

- Cut 3 strips 1½″ × WOF.
  Subcut 64 squares 1½″ × 1½″ and 3 rectangles 1½″ × 2″ for frog eyes.
- Cut 5 strips 3½″ × WOF.
  Subcut 126 rectangles 3½″ × 1½″.
- Cut 3 strips 5½″ × WOF.
  Subcut 62 rectangles 5½″ × 1½″.

GREEN:

- Cut 3 strips 1½″ × WOF.
  Subcut 62 squares 1½″ × 1½″.
- Cut 5 strips 3½″ × WOF.
  Subcut 126 rectangles 3½″ × 1½″.
- Cut 3 strips 5½″ × WOF.
  Subcut 64 rectangles 5½″ × 1½″.

RED:

- Cut 2 strips 1½″ × WOF.
  Subcut 32 squares 1½″ × 1½″.

ORANGE:

- Cut 2 strips 1½″ × WOF.
  Subcut 31 squares 1½″ × 1½″.
- Cut 4 strips 1″ × WOF for flange.

FROG GREEN:

- Cut 3 rectangles 7½″ × 10″.
- Cut 3 squares 6″ × 6″.
- Cut 3 rectangles 7″ × 8″.
- Cut 3 rectangles 3″ × 4″.

FUSIBLE INTERFACING (CHOOSE ONE):

- **C&T Wash-Away Appliqué Sheets**
  Follow the manufacturer's instructions to print 3 copies of each sheet of Hoppy patterns (pages 85 and 86) onto the *nonfusible* side of 8½″ × 11″ sheets of interfacing, using your inkjet printer.

  Note: If using C&T Wash-Away Appliqué Roll, follow the instructions for Pellon interfacing (at right).

.... *or* ....

- **Pellon 911FF Fusible Featherweight interfacing**
  Cut the interfacing into the indicated sizes and quantities of pieces listed in Flip & Fuse, Step 2 (next page). Trace the Hoppy pattern shapes (pages 85 and 86) onto the *nonfusible* side of each corresponding interfacing piece.

BORDERS:

- Cut 4 strips 5½″ × LOF for borders.

BINDING:

- Cut 6 strips 2¼″ × WOF for binding.

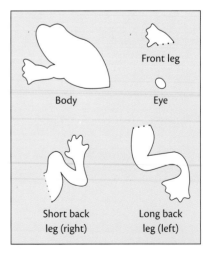

Body   Front leg

Eye

Short back leg (right)   Long back leg (left)

Flip & Fuse

For detailed instructions on this method, refer to How Flip & Fuse Works (page 5).

1. If you are using the C&T Wash-Away Appliqué Sheets, cut apart the Frog patterns. Leave at least ⅛″ beyond the drawn lines.

2. Place the following interfacing pieces on the corresponding pieces of fabric so the fusible side of the interfacing is facing the right side of the fabric.

- Place a body onto each of the 3 green 7½″ × 10″ rectangles.

- Place a short back leg onto each of the 3 green 6″ × 6″ squares.

- Place a long back leg onto each of the 3 green 7″ × 8″ rectangles.

- Place a front leg onto each of the 3 green 3″ × 4″ rectangles.

- Place an eye onto the 3 cream 1½″ × 2″ rectangles.

Fabric right side up

Interfacing glue side down

3. Sew on the lines. Do not sew on the dotted lines on the frog leg pieces. Leave these open for turning later.

4. Trim the excess fabric and fusible interfacing ⅛″ beyond the sewn lines.

Trim fabric and interfacing ⅛″ beyond stitching.

> **Tip** *For places with a tight V, such as the bend in the 2 longer frog legs, it will be easier to flip the appliqué right side out if you take 1 straight stitch across the base of the V, making a flat bottom instead of a sharp point.*

5. Cut a 2″–3″ slit in the interfacing of each piece. Cut the 2 larger leg pieces as shown.

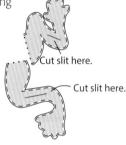
Cut slit here.

Cut slit here.

6. Flip the units right side out. Insert a blunt instrument inside the cut in the interfacing and gently push out the points and edges of each unit. Run the blunt instrument along the edges of each piece and finger-press the edges where the fabric and fusible interfacing meet. Take your time; these are difficult pieces to turn. Set the prepared pieces aside until the quilt top is constructed.

Block Construction

1. Sew cream 1½″ × 1½″ squares to 2 opposite sides of a red 1½″ × 1½″ square as shown. Press the seams toward the cream fabric. Repeat this step to make 32 units.

2. Sew cream 1½″ × 3½″ rectangles to the top and bottom of each Step 1 unit. Press the seams toward the cream fabric.

3. Sew green 1½″ × 3½″ rectangles as shown to 2 opposite sides of each Step 2 unit. Press the seams toward the green fabric.

4. Sew green 1½″ × 5½″ rectangles to the top and bottom of each Step 3 unit to make a total of 32 A blocks. Press the seams toward the green fabric.

Make 32 A blocks.

5. Repeat Steps 1–4 with the orange and green 1½″ × 1½″ squares and the remaining green and cream rectangles, following the diagram for color placement. Make a total of 31 B blocks.

Make 31 B blocks.

Quilt Top Construction

1. Sew 4 A blocks and 3 B blocks together as shown, rotating the B blocks 90° as shown, to make Row 1. Press the seams toward the A blocks. Repeat this step to make 5 rows.

Row 1

2. Sew 4 B blocks and 3 A blocks together as shown, rotating the B blocks 90° as shown, to make Row 2. Press the seams toward the A blocks. Repeat this step to make 4 rows.

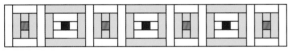

Row 2

3. Alternate Rows 1 and 2 and sew them together as shown in the quilt assembly diagram. Press all the seams in one direction.

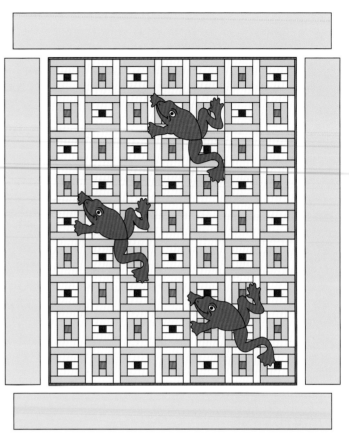

Quilt assembly

Flange and Borders

1. Sew the 4 orange 1"-wide strips together to create a long strip. Press the seams to one side.

2. Fold and press the long strip in half lengthwise, wrong sides together.

3. Measure the length of the quilt top and cut 2 flange strips to this length.

4. Measure the width of the quilt top and cut 2 more flange strips to this length.

5. Align the raw edges of a flange strip with the raw edge of one side of the quilt top and pin in place. Sew on using a stay stitch ⅛" from the raw edges. Repeat on the other side.

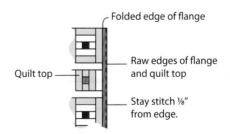

Folded edge of flange

Quilt top

Raw edges of flange and quilt top

Stay stitch ⅛" from edge.

6. Repeat Step 5 to attach the top and bottom flange strips to the quilt top.

7. Refer to *Summer Breeze*, Borders (page 13), to measure, trim, and attach first the side borders and then the top and bottom borders to the quilt top. The flange will be sandwiched between the border and the quilt top.

Adding the Frogs

1. Refer to the quilt assembly diagram (previous page) and position the 3 frog bodies on the quilt top.

2. Slide the unstitched ends of the 3 legs under the body of each frog about ¼".

3. Position the cream eyes on top of each frog body. Refer to the frog face (at right) for placement.

4. Follow the manufacturer's instructions to fuse the frogs in place, using a hot iron.

5. Using clear thread on top, sew the edge of each fused unit to the background using a blanket or zigzag stitch. Slightly lower the top tension on your machine to make sure the bobbin thread does not show on top.

6. Use a water-soluble pen to draw the mouth, nose, and eyebrow lines on each frog freehand. Refer to the frog face diagram as a guide.

7. Use dark green thread to satin stitch these facial features onto each frog.

8. Use a dark green permanent fabric-marking pen to color in the dark area of each of the frog eyes. I drew the small and large circle outlines first and then carefully colored in the dark area of each eye.

Finishing

Layer the backing, batting, and quilt top. Baste and quilt as desired. Diagonally piece the 2¼"-wide binding strips together to form a continuous strip. Trim the seam allowances to ¼" and press to one side. Press the strip in half with wrong sides together. Attach to the quilt.

Frog appliqué

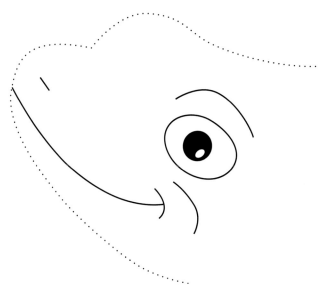

Frog face

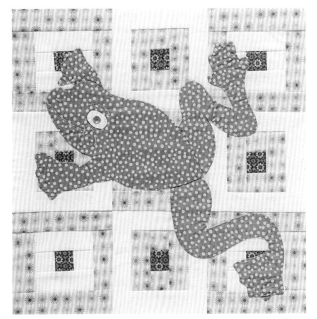

Alternate colorway

Lemon Drops

Difficulty: Level 3

Finished block: 12″ × 12″ (17″ across on point)

Finished quilt: Twin 69½″ × 88″ (size shown)

The traditional Honey Bee quilt block just got a bit sweeter with fresh, vibrant fabrics in a playful on-point setting. The Flip & Fuse appliqué is easy on this project, but the quilt top requires some piecing.

Border fabric: *Notting Hill by Joel Dewberry for FreeSpirit Fabric*

FABRIC REQUIREMENTS

Yardage is based on 42″ fabric width. An assortment of dark aqua, yellow, and mixed aqua/yellow fabrics are used to give the quilt added interest. Please refer to the suggested number of fabrics and associated yardage for *each*.

	Table runner 26½″ × 63½″	Throw 51″ × 69½″	Twin 69½″ × 88″	Queen 88″ × 88″	King 106½″ × 106½″
Number of blocks	3	8	18	25	41
Fabrics:					
White sashing	½ yard	½ yard	1 yard	1¼ yards	1¾ yards
Mixed aquas/yellows	1 fabric, ⅛ yard	3 fabrics, ⅛ yard *each*	3 fabrics, ¼ yard *each*	5 fabrics, ¼ yard *each*	5 fabrics, ¼ yard *each*
Dark aquas	3 fabrics, ¼ yard *each*	6 fabrics, ¼ yard *each*	6 fabrics, ½ yard *each*	6 fabrics, ¾ yard *each*	9 fabrics, ¾ yard *each*
Yellows	1 fabric, 1¼ yards	2 fabrics, 1½ yards *each*	3 fabrics, 1½ yards *each*	3 fabrics, 2 yards *each*	4 fabrics, 2 yards *each*
Inner border and cornerstones	⅓ yard	⅓ yard	½ yard	⅝ yard	¾ yard
Outer border (if directional print)	1¾ yards (2 yards)	1¾ yards (2½ yards)	2½ yards (3¼ yards)	2¾ yards (3½ yards)	3¼ yards (4 yards)
Binding	⅜ yard	⅝ yard	⅝ yard	¾ yard	¾ yard
Backing	2 yards	3½ yards	5½ yards	8 yards	9¾ yards
Batting	35″ × 72″	59″ × 78″	75″ × 96″	96″ × 96″	115″ × 115″
Fusible interfacing (choose one):*					
C&T Appliqué Sheets	5 sheets	10 sheets	21 sheets	29 sheets	46 sheets
Pellon 911FF	1 yard	2 yards	3½ yards	4½ yards	7½ yards

* For fusible interfacing comparisons, refer to How to Pick Your Product (page 7).

CUTTING DIRECTIONS

Each block uses 2 rectangles 3½″ × 6½″, 2 rectangles 3½″ × 12½″, and 4 squares 2½″ × 2½″ of the same fabric in either dark aqua or yellow, and 5 squares of the same mixed aqua/yellow fabric.

WOF = width of fabric; LOF = length of fabric

WHITE SASHING FABRIC:

	Table runner	Throw	Twin	Queen	King
Cut 12½″ × WOF strips.	1	1	2	3	4
Subcut 12½″ × 1½″ rectangles.	12	24	48	64	100

MIXED AQUA/YELLOW FABRICS:

	Table runner	Throw	Twin	Queen	King
Cut 2½″ × WOF strips from *each* fabric.	1	1	2	2	3
Subcut *total* of 2½″ × 2½″ squares for nine-patches.	15	40	90	125	205

DARK AQUA FABRICS:

	Table runner	Throw	Twin	Queen	King
Cut 3½" × WOF strips from *each* fabric.	1	1	2	3	3
Subcut *total* of 3½" × 6½" rectangles.	6	12	24	32	50
Subcut *total* of 3½" × 12½" rectangles.	6	12	24	32	50
Cut 2½" × WOF strips from *each* fabric.	1	1	2	3	3
Subcut *total* of 2½" × 2½" squares for nine-patches.	12	24	48	64	100
Subcut *total* of 2½" × 3½" rectangles for appliqué.	16	46	106	148	244

YELLOW FABRICS:

	Table runner	Throw	Twin	Queen	King
Cut 18¼" × 18¼" squares from *each* fabric.	1	1	1	1	1
Subcut each square twice diagonally to create side triangles.	4	6*	10*	12	16
Cut 9⅜" × 9⅜" squares from *each* fabric.	2	1	1	1	1
Subcut each square once diagonally to create corner triangles.	4	4	4*	4*	4*
Cut 3½" × WOF strips from *each* fabric.	0	1	1	2	2
Subcut *total* of 3½" × 6½" rectangles.	0	4	12	18	32
Subcut *total* of 3½" × 12½" rectangles.	0	4	12	18	32
Cut 2½" × WOF strips from *each* fabric.	3	4	5	7	8
Subcut *total* of 2½" × 2½" squares for nine-patches.	0	8	24	36	64
Subcut *total* of 2½" × 3½" rectangles for appliqué.	36	72	144	192	300

* You will have extra triangles.

DARK AQUA INNER BORDER AND CORNERSTONE FABRIC:

	Table runner	Throw	Twin	Queen	King
Cut 1½" × WOF strips.	5	6	9	10	13
Subcut 1½" × 1½" squares for cornerstones.	10	17	31	40	60

Set the remaining strips aside for the inner border.

OUTER BORDER FABRIC:

	Table runner	Throw	Twin	Queen	King
If nondirectional print:					
Cut 3½" × LOF strips.	4	—	—	—	—
Cut 6½" × LOF strips.	—	4	4	4	4
If directional print:					
Cut 3½" × WOF strips for top and bottom borders.	2	—	—	—	—
Cut 3½" × *remaining LOF* strips for side borders.	2	—	—	—	—
Cut 6½" × WOF strips for top and bottom borders.	—	3	4	5	6
Cut 6½" × *remaining LOF* strips for side borders.	—	2	2	2	2

BINDING:

	Table runner	Throw	Twin	Queen	King
Cut 2¼" × *WOF* strips.	5	8	9	10	11

FUSIBLE INTERFACING (CHOOSE ONE):

· C&T Wash-Away Appliqué Sheets

Follow the manufacturer's instructions to print the indicated number of Lemon Drops pattern sheet (page 87) onto the *nonfusible* side of 8½″ × 11″ sheets of interfacing, using your inkjet printer.

Note: If using C&T Wash-Away Appliqué Roll, follow the instructions for Pellon interfacing (at right).

C&T Appliqué Sheets	Table runner	Throw	Twin	Queen	King
Number of copies	5	10	21	29	46

···················· *or* ····················

· Pellon 911FF Fusible Featherweight interfacing

Cut the interfacing into the indicated sizes and quantities of pieces. Trace 1 shape (page 87) onto the *nonfusible* side of each corresponding interfacing piece.

Pellon 911FF	Table runner	Throw	Twin	Queen	King
Lemon drops: 2½″ × 3½″	52	118	250	340	544

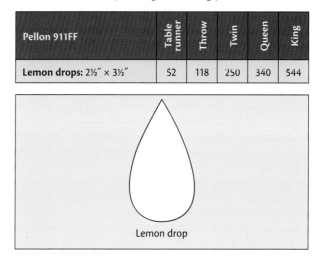

Lemon drop

Flip & Fuse

For detailed instructions on this method, refer to How Flip & Fuse Works (page 5).

1. If you are using the C&T Wash-Away Appliqué Sheets, cut apart the Lemon Drops patterns. Leave at least ⅛″ beyond the drawn lines.

2. Place the traced fusible interfacing pieces on 2½″ × 3½″ rectangles of dark aqua and yellow fabrics so that the fusible side of the interfacing is facing the right side of each fabric.

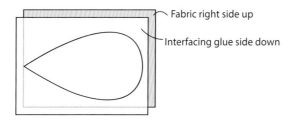

Fabric right side up

Interfacing glue side down

3. Sew on the lines.

4. Trim the excess fabric and fusible interfacing ⅛″ beyond the sewn lines.

5. Cut a slit in the interfacing of each piece, being careful not to cut the fabric.

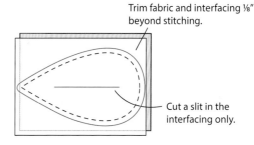

Trim fabric and interfacing ⅛″ beyond stitching.

Cut a slit in the interfacing only.

6. Flip the units right side out. Insert a blunt instrument inside the cut in the interfacing and gently push out the point and edges of each unit. Run the blunt instrument along the edges of each piece and finger-press the edges where the fabric and fusible interfacing meet. Set the prepared pieces aside until the blocks are constructed.

Block Construction

Refer to the charts (below) for the total number of blocks to make for each size quilt. *Use the same dark aqua fabric, yellow fabric, and mixed aqua/yellow fabric within a given block.*

Dark Aqua Blocks

1. Sew a dark aqua 2½" × 2½" square to each side of a mixed aqua/yellow 2½" × 2½" square. Press the seams toward the dark aqua squares.

Make 1.

2. Sew a mixed aqua/yellow 2½" × 2½" square to each side of a dark aqua 2½" × 2½" square. Press the seams toward the dark aqua square. Repeat to make a second unit.

Make 2.

3. Sew the Step 2 units to the sides of the Step 1 unit to make a nine-patch. Press the seams to one side.

4. Sew dark aqua 3½" × 6½" rectangles to 2 opposite sides of the nine-patch. Press the seams toward the dark aqua rectangles.

5. Sew dark aqua 3½" × 12½" rectangles to the top and bottom of the nine-patch. Press the seams toward the dark aqua rectangles.

6. Place 12 matching prepared light yellow lemon drop pieces on the block as shown. Follow the manufacturer's instructions to fuse in place, using a hot iron.

7. Using clear thread on top, sew the edge of each fused piece to the quilt block using a blanket stitch or a zigzag stitch. Slightly lower the top tension on your machine to make sure the bobbin thread does not show on top.

8. Repeat Steps 1–7 to make the required number of blocks.

	Table runner	Throw	Twin	Queen	King
Dark aqua blocks	3	6	12	16	25

Yellow Blocks

1. Repeat Dark Aqua Blocks, Steps 1–5, to make the indicated number of blocks with yellow and mixed aqua/yellow nine-patches and yellow rectangles as shown.

2. Repeat Dark Aqua Blocks, Steps 6 and 7, to fuse and stitch 12 matching prepared dark aqua lemon drop pieces onto each block as shown.

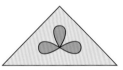

	Table runner	Throw	Twin	Queen	King
Yellow blocks	0	2	6	9	16

Side Triangles and Corners

1. Place 3 matching dark aqua lemon drop pieces on a large yellow side triangle as shown. Repeat Dark Aqua Blocks, Steps 6 and 7, to fuse and stitch the shapes onto the triangle. Repeat this step to make the required number of triangles.

	Table runner	Throw	Twin	Queen	King
Side triangles	4	6	10	12	16

2. Place a dark aqua lemon drop piece on a yellow corner triangle as shown. Repeat Dark Aqua Blocks, Steps 6 and 7, to fuse and stitch the shape onto the triangle. Repeat this step to make 4 corner triangles regardless of project size.

Quilt Top Construction

1. Lay out the dark aqua blocks, yellow blocks, white sashing, dark cornerstones, side triangles, and corner triangles in diagonal rows as shown for the selected quilt size.

2. Piece the rows together diagonally. Some rows will contain blocks, triangles, and sashing, while alternate rows will contain only sashing and posts. Press all the seams toward the sashing.

3. Sew the diagonal rows together to form the quilt top center. Be sure to line up where the posts and sashing intersect from row to row. Press all the seams toward the sashing rows.

4. Trim the posts along the edges ¼″ past the outer points of the white sashing pieces.

NOTE _____

For twin and queen size quilts, replace grayed-out blocks with side or corner triangles, as needed.

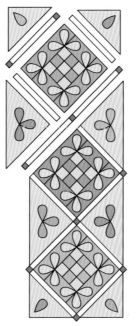

Table runner assembly

Throw quilt assembly

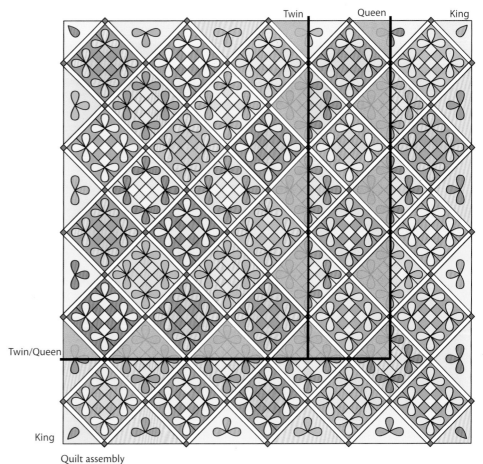

Quilt assembly

Borders

Refer to *Summer Breeze*, Borders (page 13), to make and attach the narrow inner border and then the wider outer border to the quilt top.

Finishing

Layer the backing, batting, and quilt top. Baste and quilt as desired. Diagonally piece the 2¼"-wide binding strips together to form a continuous strip. Trim the seam allowances to ¼" and press to one side. Press the strip in half with wrong sides together. Attach to the quilt.

Alternate colorway

Quilting Ideas

I love the expanding arcs Laurie Vandergriff quilted within each lemon drop. She used denser quilting in the background to make the appliqué pieces stand out. Notice the decorative line of circles within the sashing and inner border.

Coral Blossoms

Finished blocks: 16" × 16"

Finished quilt: 59" × 72"

Let a happy background fabric play in this quick weekend project. Simply add a large appliqué floral strip and you are ready to start quilting.

Fabrics: *Shades of Black and Floral Dilly Dally Grey by Me and My Sister Designs for Moda; Happy Go Lucky by Bonnie and Camille for Moda*

FABRIC REQUIREMENTS

Yardage is based on 42″ fabric width.

GRAY PRINT: 3¼ yards

DARK CORAL: 1½ yards

MEDIUM CORAL: ¼ yard

WHITE: ¾ yard

BINDING: ¾ yard

BACKING: 4¼ yards

BATTING: 67″ × 80″

FUSIBLE INTERFACING:* C&T Wash-Away Appliqué Sheets (24 sheets) *or* Pellon 911FF Fusible Featherweight interfacing (4 yards)

* For fusible interfacing comparisons, refer to How to Pick Your Product (page 7).

CUTTING DIRECTIONS

WOF = width of fabric; LOF = length of fabric

GRAY PRINT:

- Cut 2 strips 16½″ × WOF.

  Subcut 4 squares 16½″ × 16½″ and 2 rectangles 16½″ × 4½″.

- Cut the *remaining length* of the fabric on the lengthwise grain into 1 piece 13″ wide and 1 piece 29″ wide.

DARK CORAL:

- Cut 4 strips 9″ × WOF.

  Subcut 16 squares 9″ × 9″ for large circle appliqués.

- Cut 4 strips each 1½″ × WOF.

MEDIUM CORAL:

- Cut 1 strip 3″ × WOF.

  Subcut 9 squares 3″ × 3″ for small circle appliqués.

WHITE:

- Cut 4 strips 4¾″ × WOF.

  Subcut 16 rectangles 4¾″ × 9½″ for melon appliqués.

FUSIBLE INTERFACING (CHOOSE ONE):

- **C&T Wash-Away Appliqué Sheets**

  Follow the manufacturer's instructions to print 8 copies of Coral Blossom Sheet 1 and 16 copies of Coral Blossom Sheet 2 (pages 88 and 89) onto the *nonfusible* side of 8½″ × 11″ sheets of interfacing, using your inkjet printer.

  Note: If using C&T Wash-Away Appliqué Roll, follow the instructions for Pellon interfacing (at right).

  ···················· *or* ····················

BINDING:

- Cut 7 strips 2¼″ × WOF.

- **Pellon 911FF Fusible Featherweight interfacing**

  Cut the interfacing into the indicated sizes and quantities of pieces. Trace 1 shape (pages 88 and 89) onto the *nonfusible* side of each corresponding interfacing piece.

  Melons: 16 rectangles 4¾″ × 9½″

  Large circles: 16 squares 9″ × 9″

  Small circles: 9 squares 3″ × 3″

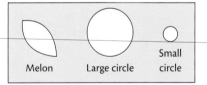

Melon   Large circle   Small circle

Flip & Fuse

For detailed instructions on this method, refer to How Flip & Fuse Works (page 5).

1. If you are using C&T Wash-Away Appliqué Sheets, cut apart the melons, large circles, and small circles. Make sure to leave at least ⅛″ beyond the drawn lines.

2. Place the fusible interfacing pieces on the corresponding pieces of fabric so the fusible side of the interfacing is facing the right side of each fabric.

- Place the melons on 4¾″ × 9½″ white rectangles.
- Place the large circles on 9″ × 9″ dark coral squares.
- Place the small circles on 3″ × 3″ medium coral squares.

3. Sew on the lines.

Fabric right side up

Interfacing glue side down

4. Trim the excess fabric and fusible interfacing ⅛″ beyond the sewn lines. Cut a slit in the interfacing of each piece, being careful not to cut the fabric.

Trim fabric and interfacing ⅛″ beyond stitching.

Cut a slit in the interfacing only.

5. Flip the units right side out. Insert a blunt instrument inside the cut in the interfacing and gently push out the points and edges of each unit. Run the blunt instrument along the edges of each piece and finger-press the edges where the fabric and fusible interfacing meet.

Block Construction

1. For the block background, fold a 16½″ × 16½″ square of gray print fabric in half vertically and horizontally. Press to crease.

2. Using the creases as a guide, place 4 large dark coral circles. Make sure the large coral circles are ¼″ in from each edge so they are not caught in the seam allowance when you sew the blocks together. Place the 4 white melons on top of the circles, with the narrower ends of each piece touching at the center of the block. The asterisk marks the narrow end.

3. Add the medium coral circle at the center of the block. Use a hot iron to fuse all the pieces in place.

4. Using clear thread on top, sew the edge of each fused piece to the background block using a blanket stitch or a zigzag stitch. Slightly lower the top tension on your machine to make sure the bobbin thread does not show on top.

5. Repeat Steps 1–4 to make a total of 4 blocks.

Quilt Top Construction

1. Sew the 4 blocks and 2 gray print 4½″ × 16½″ rectangles together as shown. Press the seams open.

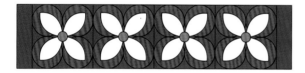

2. Position the remaining 5 medium coral small circles in the centers of the seams. Repeat Block Construction, Steps 3 and 4 (above), to fuse and stitch the circles in place.

3. Diagonally piece the 4 dark coral 1½″-wide strips to create a continuous strip. Measure the pieced strip of blocks and cut 2 dark coral strips to this length. Sew 1 strip to each side of the pieced strips. Press the seams toward the dark coral strips.

4. Cut the 13″-wide and 29″-wide gray print strips to the same length as the dark coral strips. Sew the narrower gray print strip to the left side of the pieced strip. Sew the 29″-wide gray print strip to the right side of the pieced strip. Press the seams toward the gray print strips.

Quilt assembly

Quilting Ideas

Finishing

Layer the backing, batting, and quilt top. Baste and quilt as desired. Diagonally piece the 2¼"-wide binding strips together to form a continuous strip. Trim the seam allowances to ¼" and press to one side. Press the strip in half with wrong sides together. Attach to the quilt.

Alternate colorway

Laurie Vandergriff had fun with swirls and lines within the flowers, suggesting growth and movement. However, if you use a solid background fabric, this becomes the perfect wide-open foundation for an array of quilting designs—designs that could set the mood of the quilt.

Crossroads

Finished blocks: 12″ × 12″ (17″ across on point) • **Finished quilt:** Twin 65″ × 82″ (size shown)

Fused stars add a twinkle to this pieced quilt comprised of two different main blocks. The Flip & Fuse appliqué is easy on this project, but the piecing is a little more challenging than that used in other quilts in this book.

Border fabric: *Vintage Verona by Emily Taylor Design for Riley Blake Designs*
Other fabrics: *Courtesy of Riley Blake Designs*

FABRIC REQUIREMENTS

Yardage is based on 42" fabric width.

	Runner 25" × 59"	Throw 48" × 65"	Twin 65" × 82"	Full 82" × 82"	Queen 99" × 99"	King 116" × 116"
Number of blocks	3	8	18	25	41	61
Fabrics:						
White	1 yard	1⅜ yards	2¾ yards	3½ yards	5½ yards	7¼ yards
Dark blue	¾ yard	1¼ yards	2 yards	2½ yards	3¾ yards	5 yards
Light blue	½ yard	¾ yard	1¼ yards	1½ yards	2¼ yards	2¾ yards
Green print	¾ yard	1¼ yards	2¼ yards	3 yards	4 yards	5¼ yards
Border and binding (if directional print)	1¾ yards (2 yards)	1¾ yards (2½ yards)	2¼ yards (3 yards)	2¾ yards (3 yards)	3 yards (3¾ yards)	3¾ yards (4½ yards)
Backing	2 yards	3¼ yards	5 yards	7½ yards	9 yards	10½ yards
Batting	33" × 67"	56" × 73"	73" × 90"	90" × 90"	107" × 107"	124" × 124"
Fusible interfacing (choose one):*						
C&T Appliqué Sheets	11 sheets	20 sheets	39 sheets	52 sheets	80 sheets	114 sheets
Pellon 911FF	1½ yards	3 yards	5 yards	6¾ yards	10 yards	14 yards

* For fusible interfacing comparisons, refer to How to Pick Your Product (page 7).

CUTTING DIRECTIONS

WOF = width of fabric; LOF = length of fabric

WHITE:

	Runner	Throw	Twin	Full	Queen	King
Cut 2" × WOF strips.	4	7	14	19	30	42
Subcut 2" × 12½" rectangles.	6	12	24	32	50	72
Subcut 2" × 9½" rectangles.	6	12	24	32	50	72
Cut 6" × WOF strips.	1	2	4	5	8	11
Subcut 6" × 6" squares.	3	8	18	25	41	61
Subcut 6" × 3½" rectangles.	4	6	10	12	16	20
Cut 3½" × WOF strips.	1	1	1	1	1	1
Subcut 3½" × 3½" squares.	4	4	4	4	4	4
Cut 9" × WOF strips.	1	2	3	4	7	9
Subcut 9" × 9" squares.	3	6	12	16	25	36
Cut each 9" × 9" square twice diagonally to create triangles.	12	24	48	64	100	144

DARK BLUE:

	Runner	Throw	Twin	Full	Queen	King
Cut 9½" × WOF strips.	1	2	3	4	7	9
Subcut 9½" × 9½" squares.	3	6	12	16	25	36
Cut 2" × WOF strips.	1	3	7	10	16	24
Subcut 2" × 15¼" rectangles.	0	2	6	9	16	25
Subcut 2" × 7¼" rectangles.	4	10	22	30	48	70
Cut 1¼" × WOF strips.	4	4	6	7	8	10
Subcut 1¼" × 15¼" rectangles.	4	6	10	12	16	20
Subcut 1¼" × 7" rectangles.	4	4	4	4	4	4
Subcut 1¼" × 7¾" rectangles.	4	4	4	4	4	4

LIGHT BLUE:

	Runner	Throw	Twin	Full	Queen	King
Cut 1½" × WOF strips.	8	13	21	28	40	56
Subcut 1½" × 10½" rectangles.	0	4	12	18	32	50
Subcut 1½" × 12½" rectangles.	12	20	36	46	68	94

Set the remaining strips aside for the inner border.

GREEN PRINT:

	Runner	Throw	Twin	Full	Queen	King
Cut 9" × WOF strips.	1	2	5	7	11	16
Subcut 9" × 9" squares.	3	8	18	25	41	61
Cut 5" × WOF strips.	2	2	3	4	5	6
Subcut 5" × 9" rectangles.	4	6	10	12	16	20
Subcut 5" × 5" squares.	4	4	4	4	4	4

OUTER BORDER:

	Runner	Throw	Twin	Full	Queen	King
If nondirectional print:						
Cut 3½" × LOF strips.	4	—	—	—	—	—
Cut 6½" × LOF strips.	—	4	4	4	4	4
If directional print:						
Cut 3½" × WOF strips for top and bottom borders.	2	—	—	—	—	—
Cut 3½" × remaining LOF strips for side borders.	2	—	—	—	—	—
Cut 6½" × WOF strips for top and bottom borders.	—	3	4	5	6	7
Cut 6½" × remaining LOF strips for side borders.	—	2	2	2	2	2

BINDING:

	Runner	Throw	Twin	Full	Queen	King
Cut 2¼" × remaining LOF strips.	4	4	4	4	4	4

FUSIBLE INTERFACING (CHOOSE ONE):

- ### C&T Wash-Away Appliqué Sheets

  Follow the manufacturer's instructions to print the indicated number of Crossroads pattern sheets (pages 90–93) onto the *nonfusible* side of 8½" × 11" sheets of interfacing, using your inkjet printer.

  Note: If using C&T Wash-Away Appliqué Roll, follow the instructions for Pellon interfacing (below).

C&T Appliqué Sheets	Runner	Throw	Twin	Full	Queen	King
Sheet 1	3	8	18	25	41	61
Sheet 2	2	4	9	13	21	31
Sheet 3	4	6	10	12	16	20
Sheet 4	2	2	2	2	2	2

.. or ....

- **Pellon 911FF Fusible Featherweight interfacing** Cut the interfacing into the indicated sizes and quantities of pieces. Trace 1 shape (pages 90–93) onto the *nonfusible* side of each corresponding interfacing piece. Align the dotted lines with the edges of the fusible.

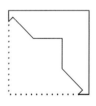

Pellon 911FF	Runner	Throw	Twin	Full	Queen	King
Large stars: 9" × 9"	3	8	18	25	41	61
Small stars: 6" × 6"	3	8	18	25	41	61
Large half-stars: 5" × 9"	4	6	10	12	16	20
Small half-stars: 3½" × 6"	4	6	10	12	16	20
Large quarter-stars: 5" × 5"	4	4	4	4	4	4
Small quarter-stars: 3½" × 3½"	4	4	4	4	4	4

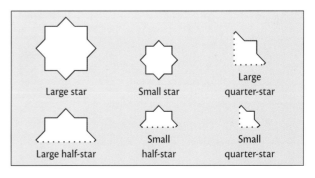

Large star Small star Large quarter-star

Large half-star Small half-star Small quarter-star

Flip & Fuse

For detailed instructions on this method, refer to How Flip & Fuse Works (page 5).

1. If you are using the C&T Wash-Away Appliqué Sheets, cut apart the Large and Small Star, Half-Star, and Quarter-Star patterns. Leave at least ⅛" beyond the solid lines and cut on the dotted lines.

2. Place each of the large star fusible interfacing pieces on a 9" × 9" square of green print fabric so the fusible side of the interfacing piece is facing the right side of the fabric.

— Fabric right side up
— Interfacing glue side down

3. Sew on the solid lines.

4. Trim the excess fabric and fusible interfacing ⅛" beyond the sewn lines.

Cut a slit in the interfacing of each piece, being careful not to cut the fabric.

— Trim fabric and interfacing ⅛" beyond stitching.
— Cut a slit in the interfacing only.

5. Flip the units right side out. Insert a blunt instrument inside the slit in the interfacing and gently push out the points and edges of each unit. Run the blunt instrument along the edges of each piece and finger-press the edges where the fabric and fusible interfacing meet. Set the prepared pieces aside until the blocks are constructed.

6. Repeat Steps 2–5 for the small stars, large and small half-stars, and large and small quarter-stars.

NOTE

Align the dotted lines on the Half-Star and Quarter-Star patterns with the raw edges of the fabric and the fusible interfacing. Stitch only on the solid lines. You do not need to cut a slit in the interfacing either; simply turn the unit right side out through the unsewn opening.

- Place the small star fusible interfacing pieces on 6" × 6" white background squares.

- Place the large half-stars on 5" × 9" green print rectangles.

- Place the small half-stars on 3½" × 6" white rectangles.

- Place the large quarter-stars on 5" × 5" green print squares.

- Place the small quarter-stars on 3½" × 3½" white squares.

Block Construction

Whole Star Blocks

1. Sew a white 2" × 9½" rectangle to each side of a dark blue 9½" × 9½" square. Press the seams toward the white rectangles.

2. Sew a white 2" × 12½" rectangle to each side of the unit made in Step 1. Press the seams toward the white rectangles.

3. *Optional: Fold the block in half vertically and horizontally and press to crease placement guides on the block. Position a green large whole star and a white small whole star on the block as shown. Follow the manufacturer's instructions to fuse in place, using a hot iron.*

Whole star block

4. Using clear thread on top, sew the edge of each fused piece to the quilt block using a blanket stitch or a zigzag stitch. Slightly lower the top tension on your machine to make sure the bobbin thread does not show on top.

5. Repeat Steps 1–4 to make the indicated number of whole star blocks for the size of quilt you are making.

	Runner	Throw	Twin	Full	Queen	King
Whole star blocks	3	6	12	16	25	36

Whole Cross Blocks

1. Sew a white triangle to each long side of a dark blue 2" × 7¼" rectangle as shown. Press the seams toward the dark blue rectangle. Refer to the chart to make the total indicated number of triangle units and set aside the indicated number for the half-cross blocks.

	Runner	Throw	Twin	Full	Queen	King
Total triangle units	4	10	22	30	48	70
Units to set aside	4	6	10	12	16	20

Note: For the table runner only, skip Steps 2–7.

2. Sew 2 units made in Step 1 to the sides of a dark blue 2" × 15¼" rectangle to make a cross block center. Press the seams toward the dark blue rectangle. Trim the center unit to 10½" × 10½" square.

3. Sew light blue 1½" × 10½" rectangles to 2 opposite sides of the center unit. Press the seams toward the light blue rectangles.

4. Sew light blue 1½" × 12½" rectangles to the remaining 2 sides of the center unit. Press the seams toward the light blue rectangles.

5. *Optional: Fold the block in half vertically and horizontally and press to crease placement guides on the block. Position a large whole green print star and a small whole white star on each block as shown. Use a hot iron to fuse in place.*

6. Stitch the appliqué units to the background block as you did for the whole star block.

7. Repeat Steps 2–6 to make the indicated number of whole cross blocks for the size of quilt you are making.

	Runner	Throw	Twin	Full	Queen	King
Whole cross blocks	0	2	6	9	16	25

Half-Cross Blocks

1. Sew a dark blue 1¼" × 15¼" rectangle to the long straight side of each remaining triangle unit.

2. Trim the dark blue strips even with the sides of the triangle units.

3. Sew a 1½" × 12½" light blue rectangle to a side of each triangle unit as shown. Press the seam toward the light blue rectangle.

4. Sew a 1½" × 12½" light blue rectangle to the adjacent side of each triangle unit. Press the seam toward the light blue rectangle. Trim the light blue strips even with the sides of the triangle units.

5. Position a large green half-star and a small white half-star on each block as shown. Use a hot iron to fuse in place.

6. Stitch the appliqué units to the background blocks as you did for previous blocks.

7. Repeat Steps 1–6 to make the indicated number of half-cross blocks for the size of quilt you are making.

	Runner	Throw	Twin	Full	Queen	King
Half-cross blocks	4	6	10	12	16	20

Quarter-Cross Blocks

Make 4 blocks for all project sizes.

1. Sew a dark blue 1¼″ × 7″ rectangle to a short side of each white triangle. Press the seam toward the dark blue rectangle.

2. Sew a dark blue 1¼″ × 7¾″ rectangle to the adjacent side of each Step 1 unit. Press the seam toward the dark blue rectangle. Trim the dark blue strips even with the side of the triangle.

3. Sew a 1½″ × 12½″ light blue rectangle to the base of each Step 2 unit. Press the

seam toward the light blue rectangle. Trim the light blue strips even with the sides of the triangle.

4. Position a large green quarter-star and a small white quarter-star on each block as shown. Use a hot iron to fuse in place.

5. Stitch the appliqué units to the background blocks as you did for previous blocks.

Quilt Top Center Construction

1. Arrange the whole star blocks, whole cross blocks, half-cross blocks, and quarter-cross blocks as shown for the selected project size. Sew the blocks together diagonally to form rows. Press all the seams toward the whole star blocks.

2. Sew the rows together diagonally as shown for the table runner and throw-size quilts to form the quilt top center. Press the seams to one side.

Table runner assembly   Throw quilt assembly

Twin-size quilt assembly

Full-size quilt assembly

Queen-size quilt assembly

King-size quilt assembly

Borders

Refer to *Summer Breeze*, Borders (page 13), to make and attach the narrow inner border and then the wider outer border to the quilt top.

Quilting Ideas

Laurie Vandergriff echoes the octagonal motif of the fused star in the center of each square block. The tulip design she selected beautifully captures the feel of the flowers in the border fabric. For the cross blocks, Laurie selected an alternate eight-sided design for the center of each star, with light airy swirls reaching outward, providing visual relief from the more dominant quilting of the square blocks.

Finishing

Layer the backing, batting, and quilt top. Baste and quilt as desired. Diagonally piece the 2¼"-wide binding strips together to form a continuous strip. Trim the seam allowances to ¼" and press to one side. Press the strip in half with wrong sides together. Attach to the quilt.

Alternate colorway

Snowflake Wallhanging

Finished quilt: 24″ × 24″ • Framed project: 28″ × 28″

Bind it or frame it! This quick quilted wallhanging will add a touch of elegance to any home.

Fabrics: *Courtesy of Hoffman Fabrics*

FABRIC REQUIREMENTS   Yardage is based on 42″ fabric width.

BLUE: 1 yard

WHITE: ¾ yard

BACKING: 1 yard

BATTING: 28″ × 28″

BINDING: ⅓ yard (needed if you do not frame the project)

FUSIBLE INTERFACING: * C&T Wash-Away Appliqué Sheets (8 sheets) *or* Pellon 911FF Fusible Featherweight interfacing (2 yards)

* For fusible interfacing comparisons, refer to How to Pick Your Product (page 7).

Optional: White 28″ × 28″ square frame with 2″ width (opening is 24″ × 24″).

CUTTING DIRECTIONS   *WOF = width of fabric; LOF = length of fabric*

BLUE:

- Cut 1 square 28″ × 28″ for background.
- Cut 8 rectangles 2½″ × 7½″.
- Cut 8 squares 2½″ × 2½″.

Optional: If you prefer to finish your project with a traditional binding rather than a frame:

- Cut 3 strips 2¼″ × WOF for binding.

WHITE:

- Cut 1 square 3″ × 3″.
- Cut 8 rectangles 3½″ × 9½″.
- Cut 8 rectangles 3″ × 4½″.
- Cut 8 rectangles 3½″ × 4½″.

FUSIBLE INTERFACING (CHOOSE ONE):

- **C&T Wash-Away Appliqué Sheets**
Follow the manufacturer's instructions to print 8 Snowflake pattern sheets (page 94) onto the *nonfusible* side of 8½″ × 11″ sheets of interfacing, using your inkjet printer.

Note: If using C&T Wash-Away Appliqué Roll, follow the instructions for Pellon interfacing (at right).

.... *or* ....

- **Pellon 911FF Fusible Featherweight interfacing**   Cut the interfacing into the indicated sizes and quantities of pieces. Trace 1 shape (page 94) onto the *nonfusible* side of each corresponding interfacing piece.

A: Cut 1 square 3″ × 3″.

B: Cut 8 rectangles 3½″ × 9½″.

C: Cut 8 rectangles 2½″ × 7½″.

D: Cut 8 rectangles 3″ × 4½″.

E: Cut 8 rectangles 3½″ × 4½″.

F: Cut 8 squares 2½″ × 2½″.

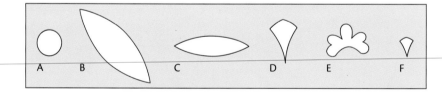

Flip & Fuse

For detailed instructions on this method, refer to How Flip & Fuse Works (page 5).

1. If you are using the C&T Wash-Away Appliqué Sheets, cut apart the Snowflake patterns. Leave at least ⅛″ beyond the drawn lines.

2. Place each F fusible interfacing piece on a 2½″ × 2½″ blue square so the fusible side of the interfacing is touching the right side of the fabric.

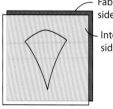

Fabric right side up

Interfacing glue side down

3. Sew on the lines.

4. Trim the excess fabric and fusible interfacing ⅛″ beyond the sewn lines.

5. Cut a slit in the interfacing of each piece, being careful not to cut the fabric.

Trim fabric and interfacing ⅛″ beyond stitching.

Cut a slit in the interfacing only.

6. Flip the units right side out. Insert a blunt instrument inside the cut in the interfacing and gently push out the points and edges of each unit. Run the blunt instrument along the edges of each piece and finger-press the edges where the fabric and fusible interfacing meet.

7. Repeat Steps 2–6 for the remaining shapes.

- Place the A fusible interfacing piece on the 3″ × 3″ white square.

- Place the B fusible interfacing pieces on 3½″ × 9½″ white rectangles.

- Place the C fusible interfacing pieces on 2½″ × 7½″ blue rectangles.

- Place the D fusible interfacing pieces on 3″ × 4½″ white rectangles.

- Place the E fusible interfacing pieces on 3½″ × 4½″ white rectangles.

Tip *For places with a tight V, like the E shape here, it will be easier to flip the appliqué right side out if you take 1 straight stitch across the base of the V, making a flat bottom instead of a sharp point.*

Assembly

1. Fold the blue background square in half vertically and horizontally. Press to crease.

2. Using the creased guidelines, place the white circle A in the center of the background square and use a hot iron to fuse in place.

3. Position the white large melon B pieces around the center circle as shown. Fuse in place.

4. Center the blue small melon C piece on top of the white melons. Fuse in place.

5. Position the white D and E pieces in between the B and C melon pieces as shown. Fuse in place.

6. Position the blue F pieces on top of the white D pieces and fuse in place.

7. Using clear thread on top, sew the edge of each fused piece to the background block using a blanket stitch or a zigzag stitch. Slightly lower the top tension on your machine to make sure the bobbin thread does not show on top.

Finishing

Layer the backing, batting, and quilt top. Baste and quilt as desired. Place directly in the white frame *or* trim to a 24″ × 24″ square and apply a traditional binding.

Alternate colorway

Patterns

Summer Breeze Patterns—Sheet 1

Seam allowances are *not* included on patterns.

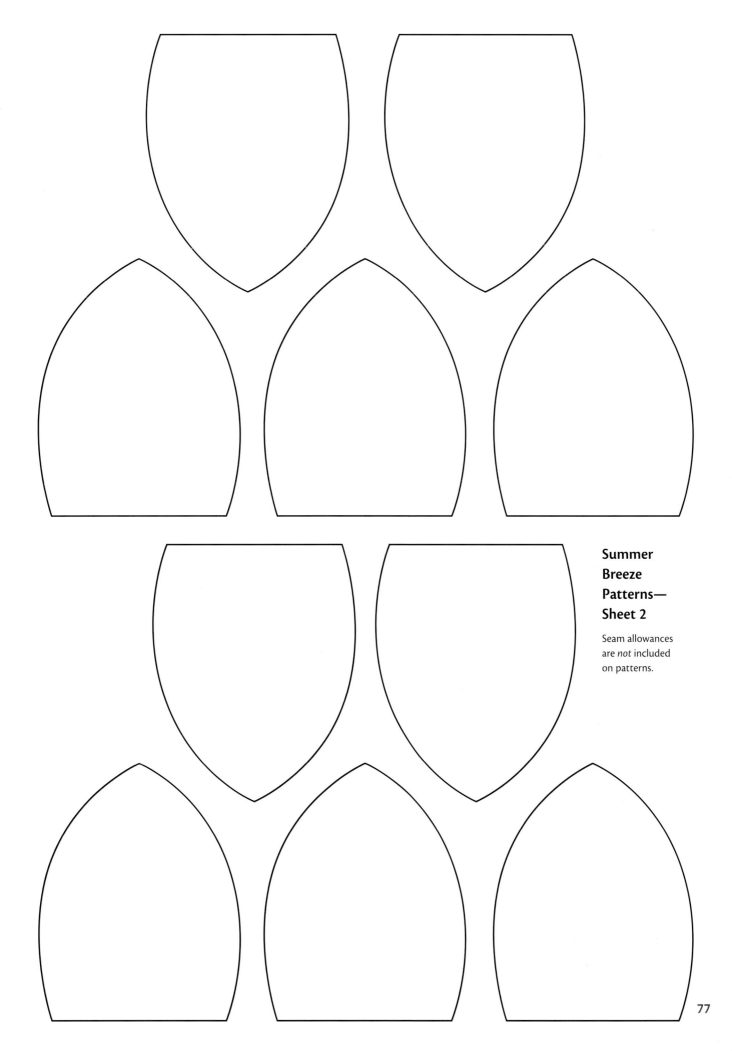

Summer Breeze Patterns— Sheet 2

Seam allowances are *not* included on patterns.

77

Petal Patch Patterns

Seam allowances are *not* included on patterns.

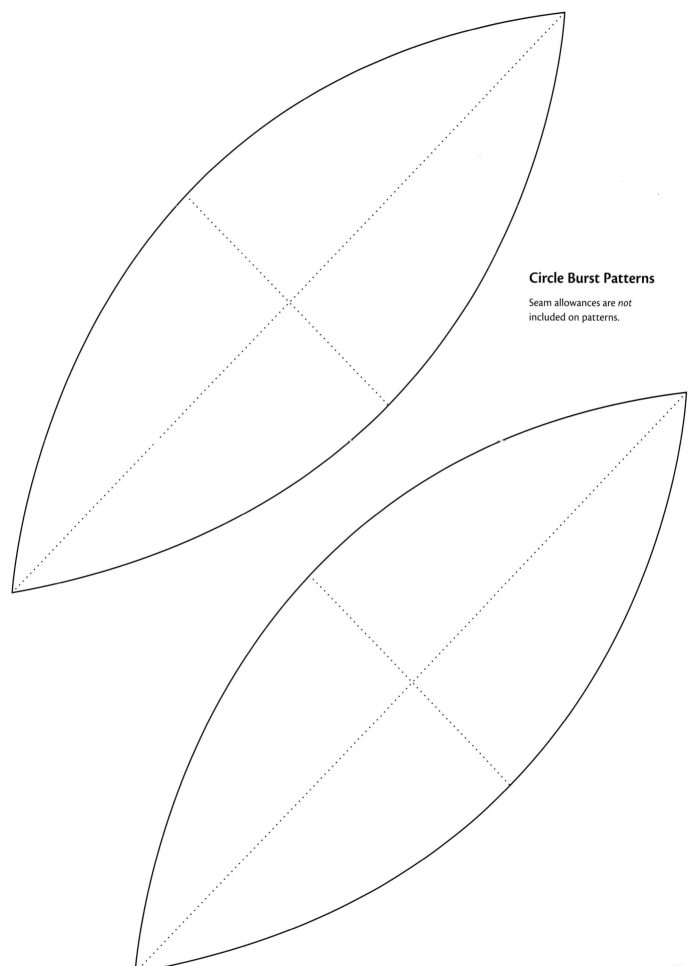

Circle Burst Patterns

Seam allowances are *not* included on patterns.

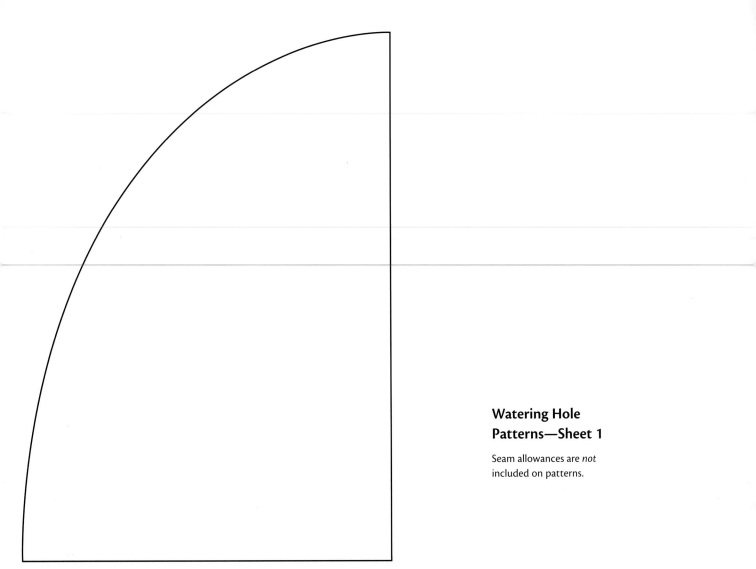

Watering Hole
Patterns—Sheet 1

Seam allowances are *not* included on patterns.

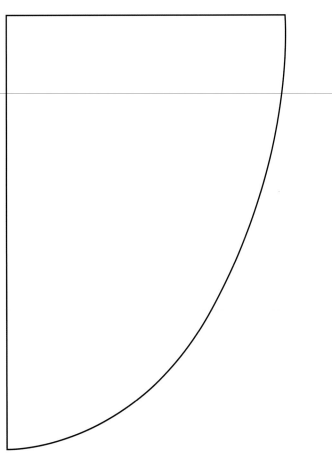

**Watering Hole
Patterns—Sheet 2**

Seam allowances are *not*
included on patterns.

R = Reversed   R   R   R = Reversed

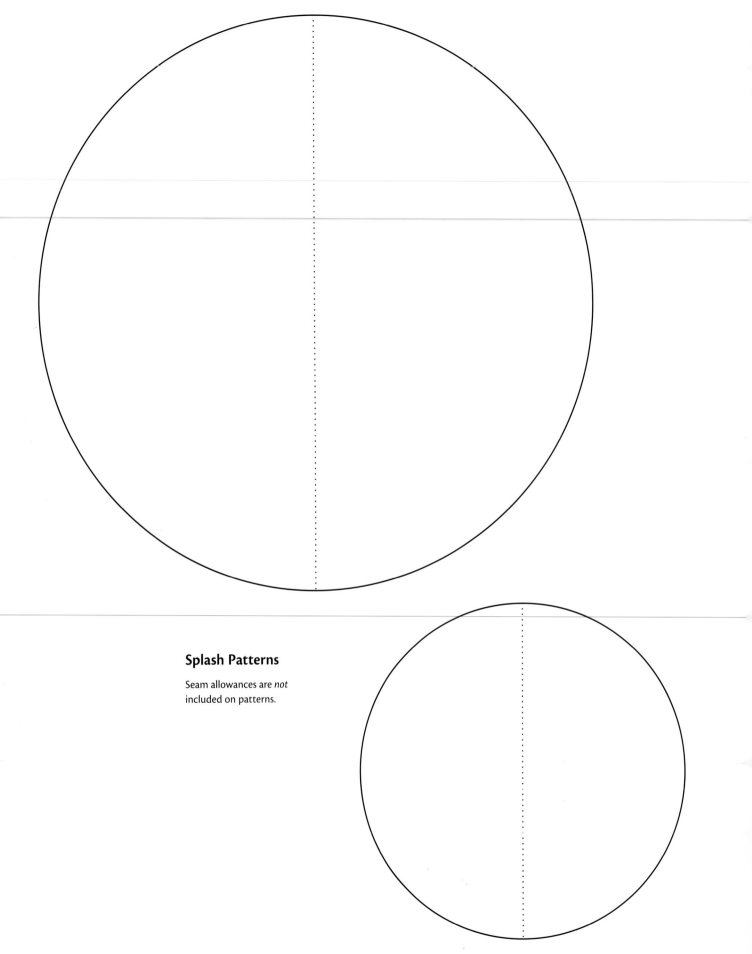

Splash Patterns

Seam allowances are *not*
included on patterns.

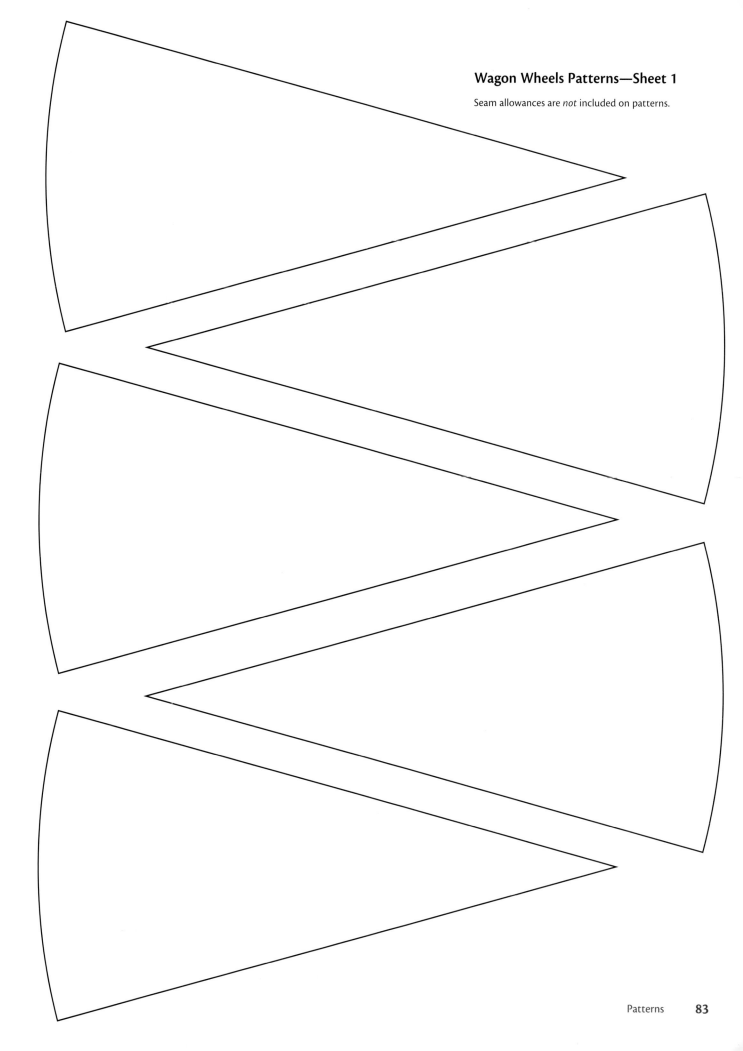

Wagon Wheels Patterns—Sheet 1

Seam allowances are *not* included on patterns.

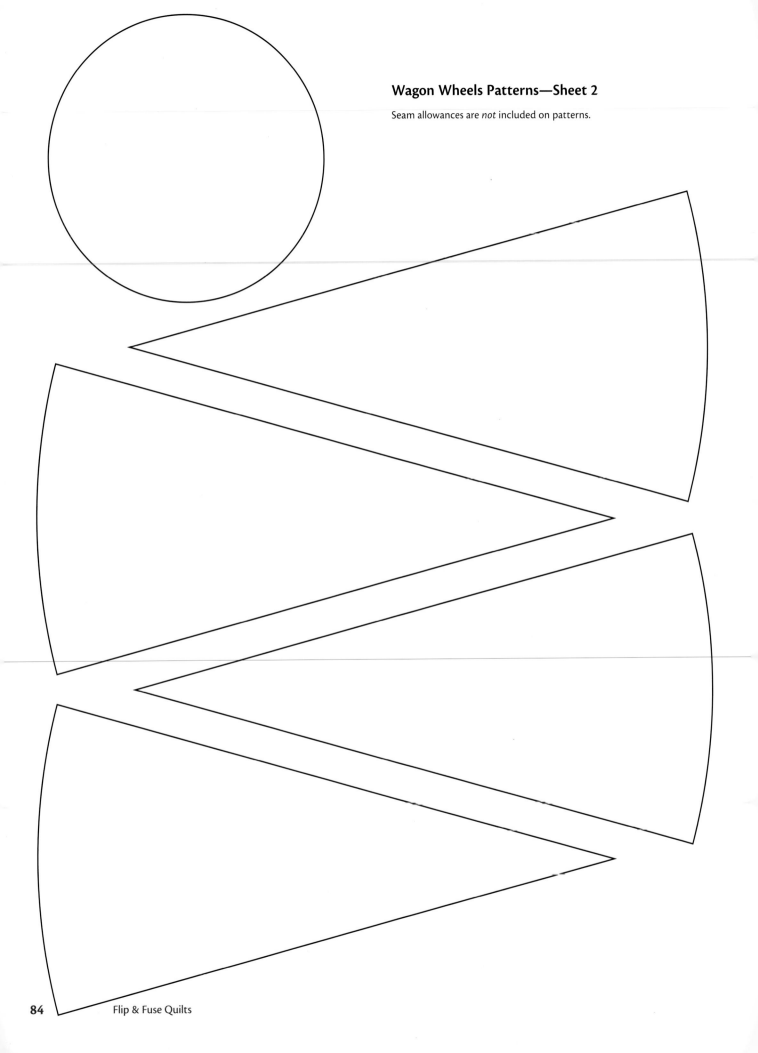

Hoppy Patterns—Sheet 1

Seam allowances are *not* included on patterns.

Hoppy Patterns—Sheet 2

Seam allowances are *not* included on patterns.

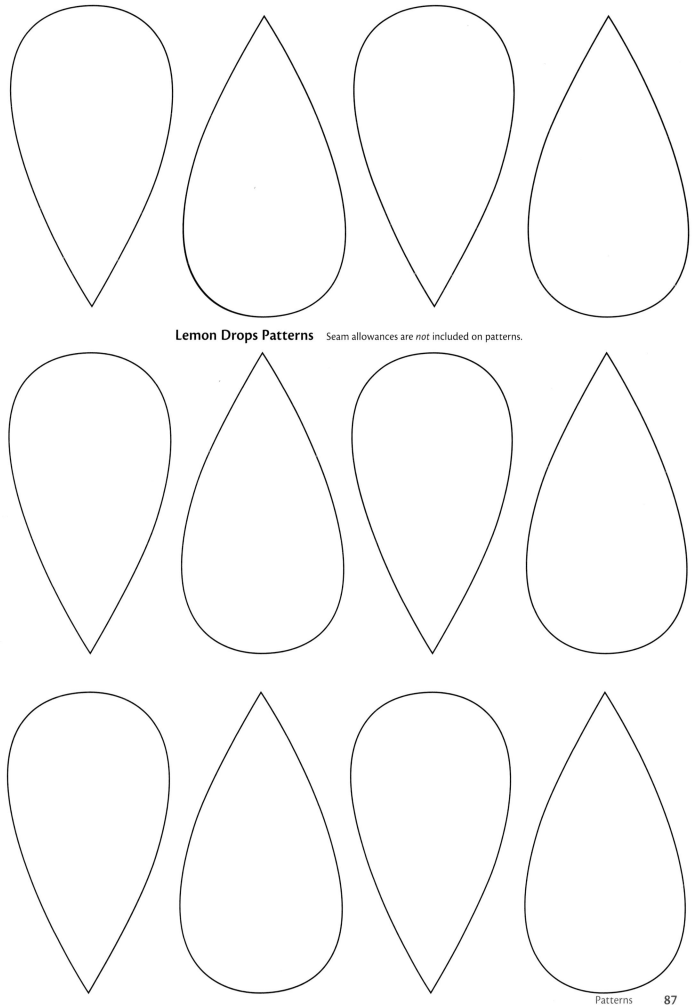

Lemon Drops Patterns Seam allowances are *not* included on patterns.

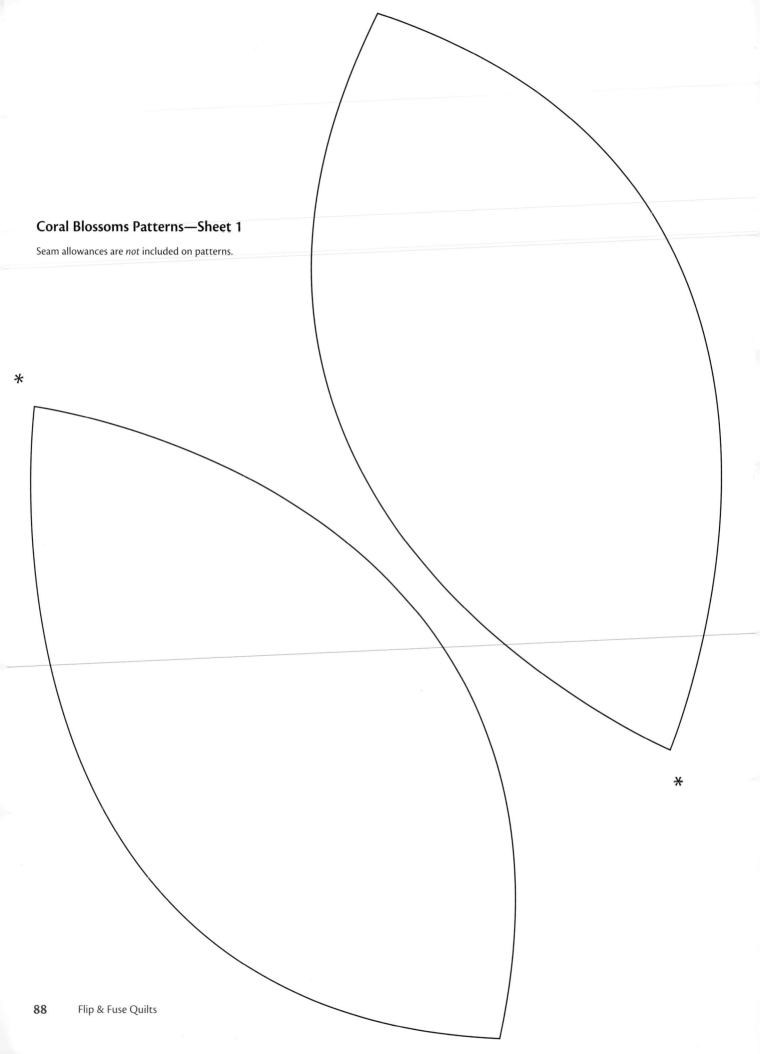

Coral Blossoms Patterns—Sheet 1

Seam allowances are *not* included on patterns.

*

*

Coral Blossoms Patterns—Sheet 2

Seam allowances are *not* included on patterns.

Seam allowances are *not* included on patterns.

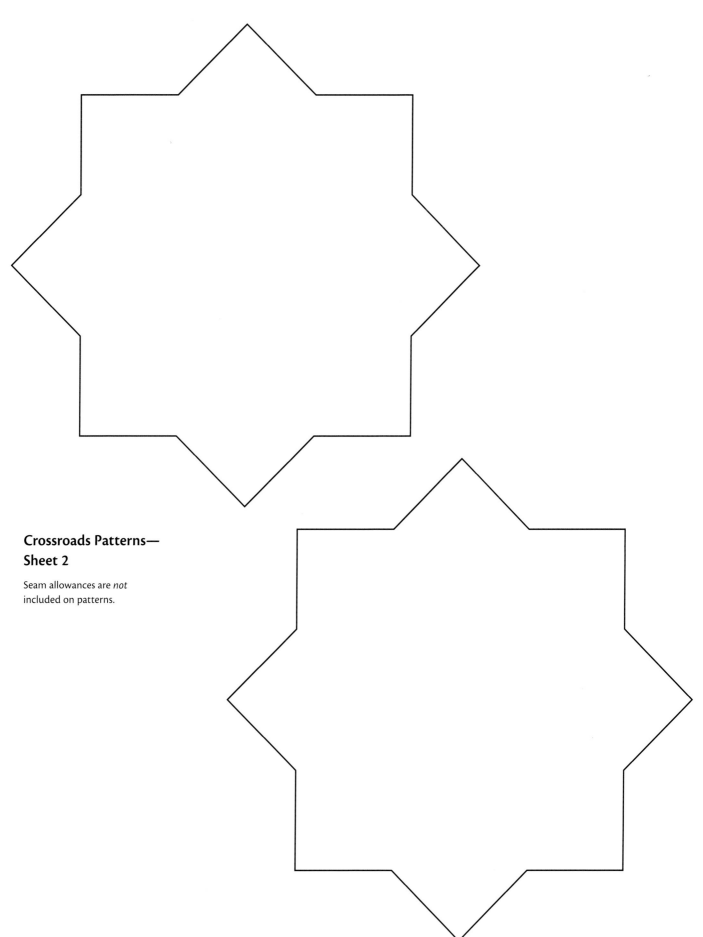

**Crossroads Patterns—
Sheet 2**

Seam allowances are *not* included on patterns.

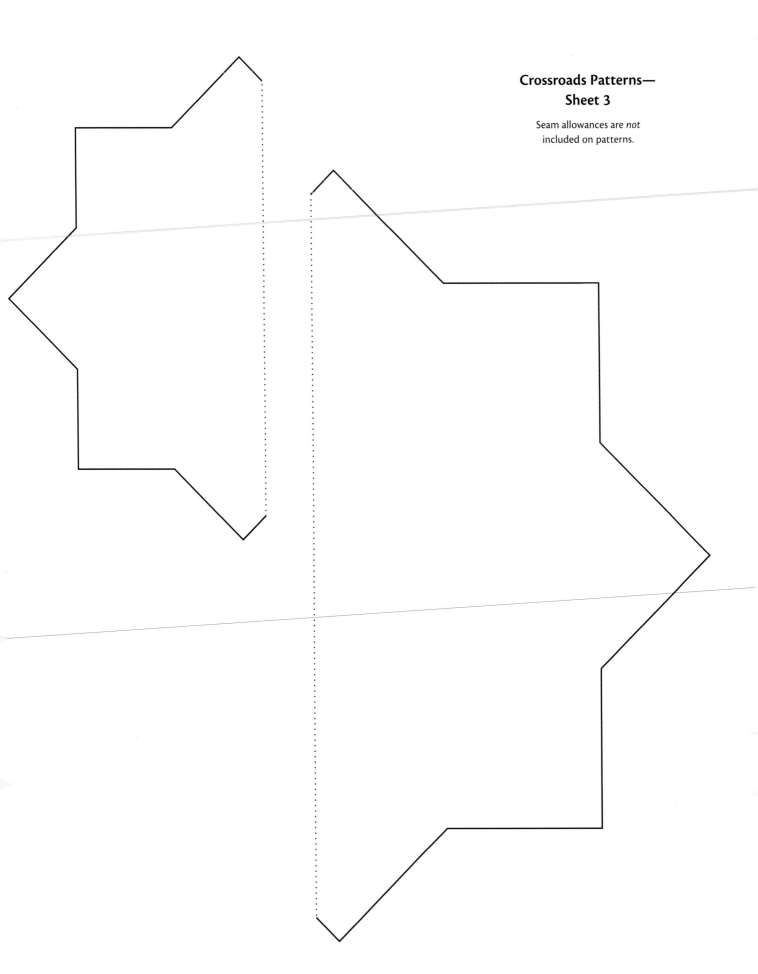

**Crossroads Patterns—
Sheet 3**

Seam allowances are *not*
included on patterns.

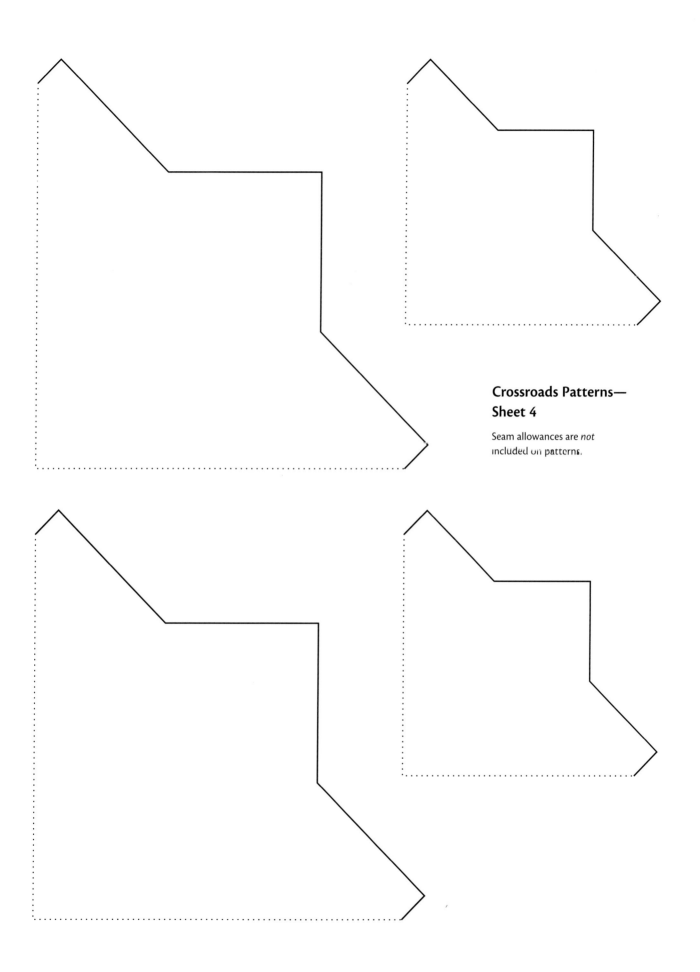

**Crossroads Patterns—
Sheet 4**

Seam allowances are *not* included on patterns.

Snowflake Patterns

Seam allowances are *not* included on patterns.

A

B

D

F

E

C

About the Quilters

Meet the Author

Photo by Darby Ann Photography

MARCIA HARMENING of Happy Stash Quilts lives in Reno, Nevada, with her husband, Mike, and youngest daughter, Robin. She is a quilt pattern designer, lecturer, and instructor.

Marcia fell in love with quilting twenty years ago as a means of staving off insanity during the long, dark Alaska winters. She found that colorful fabric combined with colorful friendships is, indeed, the perfect solution for surviving the snowy, monochromatic season. In 2010, after 23 years in Alaska, Marcia, her husband, and their three children relocated to Reno, where they are soaking in an unbelievable abundance of sunshine.

Marcia has more than 50 patterns and two other books in publication. Her work appears regularly in quilting magazines. See her complete collection at happystashquilts.com.

Meet the Longarmer

Photo by Alexander Vandergriff

LAURIE VANDERGRIFF of Spring Creek Quilting worked her amazing longarm magic on every quilt in this book. Laurie lives in Manteno, Illinois, where she enjoys spending time with her children— Jessica, Rachel, Holly, and Alexander—and a menagerie of four-legged, feathered, and finned friends. When she is not camping, fishing, or riding four-wheelers with the family, you can find Laurie quilting, knitting, crocheting, and making doilies. Her inspiration comes from her mother, Gloria Bolling, who is also a longarm quilter. Laurie is a member of the Kankakee Quiltmakers Guild.

Resources

Fusible Interfacing

C&T Wash-Away Appliqué Sheets and Wash-Away Appliqué Roll
C&T Publishing
ctpub.com

Pellon 911FF Fusible Featherweight interfacing
Pellon
pellonprojects.com
Available at most craft stores and quilt shops

Fabric

These companies generously provided fabric used in quilts in this book:

FreeSpirit Fabric
freespiritfabric.com

Hoffman Fabrics
hoffmanfabrics.com

Michael Miller Fabrics
michaelmillerfabrics.com

Moda
unitednotions.com

Riley Blake Designs
rileyblakedesigns.com

Timeless Treasures
ttfabrics.com